BE*coming* PaRVAti

A Modern Exploration of the Yamas & Niyamas

BY JULIE A. HILLMAN

BEcoming ParVAti ©2020

All rights reserved. No part of this book may be reproduced or transmitted in any form or by any means, electronic or mechanical, including photocopying, recording, or by any information storage and retrieval systems, without permission in writing from the author.

Paperback IBSN: 978-0-578-67235-9

Julie A. Hillman
28 Sheffield Ave
North Providence, RI 02911
www.satya-wellness.com

IN graTItude

There are so many people who, without their role in my life, this book would never have happened. I will never be able to thank you all individually here, but I trust that you know who you are.

I first thank my husband, Ian, for his love and support. Thank you for sharing this life with me, for growing together.

Special thanks to Sara L. Brandon for her amazing artwork.

Gratitude to Swami Kripalu for his dedication to Sadhana.

Thank you, Shri Amrit Desai, for your dedication to the yogic teachings and for bringing them out into the world. Without your work I would not have gained the knowledge, understanding, or experience that I have now. Thank you for sharing this with the teachers you have trained, for they have been my mentors and have helped to reveal the meaning of yoga.

Thank you to my yoga students. As you learn, I learn. As you grow, I grow. Thank you for keeping me on my path Thank you for sharing the path with me.

Last, but never least, a very special thank you, Griffon. You will always be a part of my heart.

CONTENTS

INTRODUCTION 6

THE YAMAS 13

APARIGRAHA 14

ASTEYA 32

BRAHMACHARYA 40

AHIMSA 48

SATYA 58

THE NIYAMAS 67

SANTOSHA 68

SAUCHA 78

TAPAS 84

SWADHYAYA 92

ISHVARA PRANIDHANA 98

BECOMING PARVATI 106

MOVING FORWARD 118

RESOURCES 124

ABOUT THE AUTHOR 125

INTRO_duction_

I remember seeing this book – All I need to know I learned from my Cat (Becker 1990). I never read it, but it's one of those books that are supposed to illustrate the simpleness of life, often through funny quips and stories. I didn't learn everything from my cat, but one of the most lasting, impressive lessons in my life was learned through her.

Griffon passed on March 29, 2018. I remember the day well. She had been sick the day before. She was sleeping at the end of my bed, as she did every night. I felt her stirring and woke to tend to her. Her breathing was labored, she had difficulty moving, and she was shifting her position to be with each of her toys (small stuffed toys, her "babies," that we kept at the end of the bed for her). I knew what she was doing. She also climbed on top of my husband's legs, which she never did in all of her eighteen-plus years; after her visit with him she struggled to find a comfortable position. I took her in my arms, lay down with her, and covered us in blankets. I held her close, whispered to her. Her breath was labored, her body trembled. I knew these would be my last moments with her.

In the midst of this, I remember hearing (in my mind) the voice of my teacher saying, very definitively: Aparigraha. And when I ignored it, it was there again: Aparigraha.

Aparigraha. Non-attachment, non-hoarding. In this moment I knew this meant to stop holding on and let Grif-

fon go. So, I told her I would be okay – that I would miss her and her cuddles, but I would be okay – and if she needed to let go to do so. I told her I loved her. I felt the tensions ease in her body and, after some time, I felt her last breath as I held her close
to me.

So, you might be wondering, what does this have to do with yoga? Well, in essence, everything.

Aparigraha is one of the yamas, or observances, set forth in the Yoga Sutras. In a sense, the yamas, combined with the niyamas (disciplines), serve as guidelines for living a spiritual life. I consider them to be a sort of "Ten Commandments," if you will. So when I heard my teacher's voice say, "Aparigraha", it hit me hard.

Let me paint a little more of this picture. I adopted my cat, Griffon, when she was a barely weaned kitten; she was almost 19 when she passed. She loved to be in the company of my husband and me. Her favorite places were outside in the sunny garden or curled up in our blankets. The last couple years of her life I found, more often than not, that my daily schedule revolved around her and her increasing medical needs (chronic kidney disease and, eventually, lymphoma). Honestly, my daily life revolved around her needs much like a parent around their sick child. And in the early hours of March 29 I wanted nothing more than to keep this being as comfortable as possible. It was all about her.

But at the same time, I was already anticipating the

loss. She can't leave me, what will I do? She was like my child – what will be my purpose after this?

I didn't think about these questions consciously, the knowledge was just there. Just as the voice coming to me, telling me to let go. When I listened to the words – Aparigraha, Aparigraha – and felt their true meaning, a sense of total peace came over me at that moment. I was still incredibly sad and beginning to grieve, but there was a sense of ease and peace.

This experience is what inspired me to write this book. Though this was a deeply sad time for me, I had a sense of a viscerally deep understanding – a knowing – of what aparigraha was. It was during the weeks immediately following Griffon's death that I explored my grief as well as looking at how my yoga practice supported me during this time. It wasn't the asana (postures) that supported me, but the scriptural teachings. The teachings provided me with a foundational skill set that I could use any time in my life, but they proved especially useful when I needed extra strength. I wanted to share my knowledge of these tools so that others could benefit from them. Thus, Becoming Parvati was born.

the yamas and niyamas are the first two steps of the eight-limbed yogic path set forth by the great sage Patanjali. These limbs are yama (disciplines, abstinence), niyama (observances), asana (the physical postures or poses), pranayama (breath control), pratyahara (sense withdrawal, inward focus), dharana (concentration), dyana (meditation), and Samadhi (contemplation, absorption, super- conscious state). These eight limbs are not sequential, but are to be practiced simultaneously. It is through the consistent practice of yoga (referring to all eight limbs, not just asana) that a spiritual seeker is able to re-discover their true Self.

This book is specifically focusing on the yamas and niyamas because they are practices for anyone on any path to contemplate, understand and utilize. There are also great depth and layers of meaning to be discovered in just these two limbs. "The purity of body, mind and heart that we achieve from the practice of the yamas and niyamas reveals the unconscious patterns of our self-image and self-concepts" (Desai 49). Wholeheartedly studying the yamas and niyamas, putting them into practice, and contemplating their deepest meanings can be profoundly healing to anyone on any spiritual or religious path.

There are five yamas and five niyamas. Yamas consist of ahimsa (non- harming), satya (truth), asteya (non-stealing), brahmacharya (moderation), and aparigraha. The niyamas are saucha (purity), santosha (contentment), tapas (spiritual heat), swadhyaya (spiritual study), and Ishvara pranidhana (surrender or dedication to god). In The Yoga Sutras of Patanjali they are addressed in this order specifically. I believe it is because the first of the yamas and niyamas – ahimsa and saucha – promote the proper mindset for study and practice. You must make a vow to do no harm in the process of your study and you must be pure of heart and thought in order for the truest and deepest meanings of any spiritual practice to be fully discovered.

However, you will find in this book that I strayed from this tradition. In part this is because it reflects the order in which I was inspired to write; in part because it simply seemed to make sense. You will also find that my approach is different than many texts on this topic. These teachings date back over two thousand years. Although the heart and soul of these teachings remain relevant today – perhaps even more so – much has changed in terms of general lifestyle, so the ancient examples may no longer be relevant in today's society. It is through my personal practice and study that I have come to this understanding of the yamas and niyamas, and it is through this understanding that I present this book using examples from modern life, applying the teaching of each yama and niyamas in a practical way. Additionally, each chapter begins with a definition of the yama or niyama as well as the relevant sutra (line or stanza) from The Yoga Sutras of Pantanjali.

It is my intent to provide a modern perspective on the teaching of the yamas and niyamas. A perspective that does not require you to have an established yoga practice, or any knowledge of yoga whatsoever. It is my wish that something on the following pages resonates with you, and that the meaning of each sutra will be illustrated in a way that makes these teachings more relevant to your life at this, and every, moment.

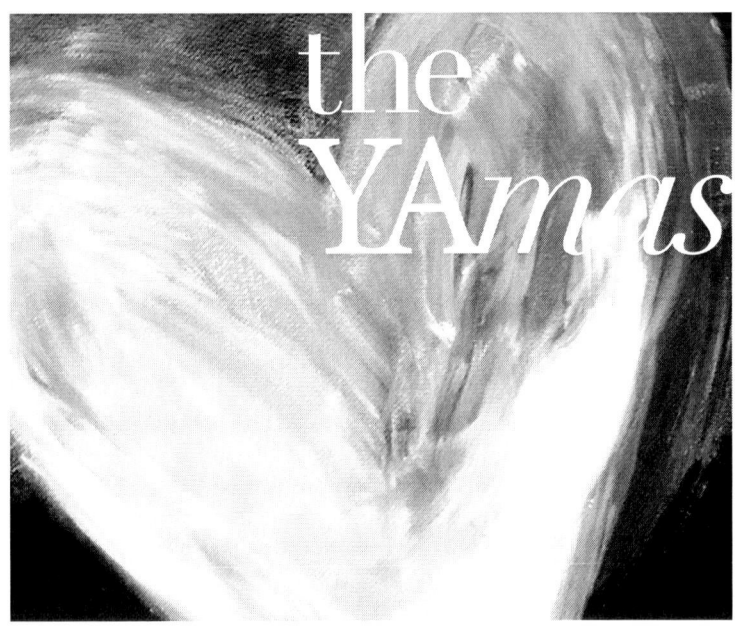

the Yamas

[YAH-maas]
Sutra 2:30

Yama consists of
non-violence,
truthfulness,
non- stealing,
continence,
and non-greed

the YA*mas*

[a-PARI-grah-ha]

Meaning
non-attachment,
non-hoarding

Sutra 2:39
*When non-greed is confirmed,
a thorough illumination
of the how and the why
of one's birth comes.*

In most Western societies, we are taught from an early age that our possessions speak for how well we are doing in life. How big your house is, how many cars, what type of cars, how big is your bank account? Your answers to these questions will tell you how well you are you are doing, how secure you are. I imagine that this was also true in our ancient history, though instead of cars we may have been judged by how many cows we had.

I remember being teased for the clothes I wore in grade school. I don't remember my family struggling financially, but we were definitely not considered "rich." We shopped at discount department stores like Walmart (before Walmart was a thing). I don't think I owned a brand name clothing item until I was in college, quite honestly. My classmates, many of whom came from families that had more money, wore the latest brand-name fashions. But it wasn't about what I had; it was about what I lacked. I appeared to lack the resources to purchase "good" clothing, and my peers reacted by teasing. I was being conditioned to know that the quality of my possessions, in this case clothing, would indicate my status in society.

As adults this is still the case. Take a drive through a neighborhood that you've never been to, what do you do? You look at the houses – size, style, the grounds, are there boarded-up houses, garbage in the streets. You look at the driveways – do you see a bunch of luxury cars or do you see beat-up old Chevy's. Are the lawns bright green and perfectly manicured, well-cared for but not perfect, or is everything overgrown? This is how you begin to form your opinions about the people who live in those houses, whether this is a "good" neighborhood or a "bad" one. You are placing a value on the neighborhood and its residents based on the quantity and quality of the possessions you see.

It is our fears that drive us to accumulate objects of desire. It gives us a sense of safety and control, a sense of belonging. My guru wrote "basically, all attachments are the representation of unconscious fears. Our addictions to our possessions, which we call security, actually represent our insecurity, fear and greed. All hoarding and clinging are fear and security-based" (Desai p55). We have a desire to be accepted by others, we have a desire to be successful. Many of us only know how to determine our success and security by the possessions we have. So the more successful we think we are the more things we acquire. Then, as we are more successful we trade those for better things – better cars, bigger houses. Our peers admire us for our successes in life evidenced by what we have.

But what if that beautiful house is gone tomorrow? Let's say my house is destroyed in a fire. That does not mean I am any less successful; but that house represents my success, my security. I no longer have a means of showing my success, not only to my peers but to myself as well. And if I am not able to rebuild my home to the same – or better – level of beauty and comfort, it will only appear to illuminate a lack of success, which is what I fear. We mistakenly put value into the things themselves rather than the value on the emotional construct. The emotional construct will always be present. It is the joys, security, freedom, status that we have obtained from our efforts in life. These joys, securities, freedoms, and status are what have afforded us the ability to obtain those objects of desire. It's a case of mistaken identity.

Perhaps an easier way to understand how our attachment to things is a representation of our fears is to imagine that as a child your family never had stable housing. Every year, or more frequently, your family moved from apartment to apartment; perhaps different towns or states. You would become anxious about when the next move would be. As an adult, as soon as you were able you purchased a house. Someplace stable. Someplace you wouldn't have to leave. This house isn't just a place to raise your family, it represents the stability you didn't have as a child. And now that you have it, you will worry that you will lose it. It may sit way in the back of your mind, perhaps just a feeling or sense without a name; but you will become attached to that house and the security it represents because you fear losing that stability.

All of this is completely subconscious, of course. We don't go around saying "I want this expensive item

17

so everyone knows that I have my shit together, and so I can convince myself that I have my shit together." Yes, we feel a sense of accomplishment when we have the ability to make a purchase we couldn't afford previously. Yes, we like the accolades and recognition that we have done well. We don't think about the achievements until we need to let things go.

Imagine you are cleaning out a closet. You get to the very back of it, maybe high on a shelf. You pull out a box of items that you have long forgotten you even had. So you start going through that box. You find some old jewelry that you obviously never wear. You consider giving it to a niece, but it was given to you for your first communion so there is sentimental value attached. Perhaps you find your deceased grandfather's service pistol. Even though you don't want weapons in your house, you have kept the pistol because you feel it would be disrespectful to your grandfather's memory to sell the weapon. You find an old pair of jeans. These were your favorite, and so soft and comfortable. But now they are two sizes too small, but you have kept them anyhow "just in case" you fit into them again. I am sure you can relate to these, even if the exact examples do not apply directly to your life. These examples show attachment to the things. And we are afraid that we will forget that feeling of sacredness if we gave away our cross pendant. We will tarnish fond memories if we sell a gun. Perhaps we are afraid our motivation to exercise more will be diminished if we don't have our old too small pants to motivate us. In reading this we may laugh at how funny it sounds, but we all do this. We mistakenly put our sentiments onto the things rather than what they represent.

I am not telling you to get rid of all of your things, but to begin releasing attachment to them. Begin by going through a section of your house – a closet perhaps – and looking at each object. Are there sentiments attached? What are they? Do they bring back memories? Then consider throwing that item away. Does that bring a sudden sense of anxiety, fear? Why? Start to look at why you have those feeling and really look at what brought you the joy – the memories or the item? The item may have sparked the memories, but the memories
were there with or without the item. Then, keep the item if you want, or let it go if the time is right. Beginning to sever the attachment to the items, setting the path toward greater freedom physically, emotionally and spiritually.

We are a very goal-oriented society. We are taught the importance of goals very young in life. Get good grades, do well in sports, get a good paying job, start a family. In our professional lives our compensation structure is based on, among other things, our place in the hierarchy. We receive greater benefits as we promote, so we are in a constant race to the next higher position in our companies. And we are led to believe that when we achieve these benchmarks, we will find happiness.

Goals can be of a personal nature. Wanting to

reach a certain weight, level of fitness, obtaining the dream home or car. Perhaps they are a way of marking progress on a particular journey. Goals can keep us on that path. But they can also wreak havoc with our self-esteem and self- value.

Have you ever wanted something so badly that you would do almost anything to get it? Let's be honest, I have. Maybe it's a certain job or position, a car, an expensive piece of jewelry. And you work really hard to get it; and as you work toward obtaining this thing, your goal, you're thinking about how great you're going to feel when you finally get it. And the day finally comes, you get this thing you've been working so hard for and you feel great in that moment, but… it's fleeting. And soon it no longer brings you joy, so you seek out something else. Been there? I certainly have. So what happened?

In this heavily goal-oriented society we are constantly placing our happiness "out there," sometime in the future. We have learned that happiness lies in obtaining certain things, making so much money, having so many children, etc. We are accustomed to placing happiness upon some future outcome. And when we achieve that outcome either it doesn't bring the joy we expected or it no longer fits our needs.

Real happiness resides in being happy now, in the present moment. We can still work toward our goals or the attainment of things – in fact we should because it keeps us motivated and productive – but do not wait until the attainment of these things to find happiness and contentment, My teacher, Amrit Desai, has said we have the right to take action, but we do not have the right to the fruit of those actions. In other words, we can take appropriate actions – in this case, to work toward a specific goal – be we cannot become attached to obtaining a specific result.

In a practical sense, let's continue with the example of growing in your job. Imagine that you are working to be promoted to manager in your department. You work really, really hard and put in a lot of hours. Then you find out you did not get the management position, a coworker did. You are so devastated that you immediately resign from the company. Your boss accepts your resignation and you pack your belongings. On your way out the door, your boss states that he's sad to see you leave because you would have been an excellent Vice President: you didn't get the management position because you were going to be promoted to Vice President. We can say that all your happiness was contingent upon obtaining the management position; so when you did not obtain that position you felt unhappy and unsatisfied. You were so attached to that specific outcome that you missed out on an opportunity that could have had greater benefit, and perhaps greater joy. If you found contentment in everyday while working toward your goal, you would have remained happy even without the management position (okay, you would have been momentarily disappointed, but your overall happiness would remain); you would not have been prompted to make the quick decision to quit your job, and you would have found yourself the Vice President of your company. In other words, we can – and should – plan and work toward future achievements, but we should not be held so fast to a specific outcome. When we can release our attachment to a specific outcome, more often than not we find an opportunity far greater than we first imagined.

another example of attachment to outcomes, or results, happened between myself and one of my students Steve has been a regular and dedicated student for a few years now. He comes to class every week, has read and studied recommended books, and asks deeply probing questions on yogic philosophy. And yet, to my chagrin, he has had no desire to immerse himself in a few days of yoga at the ashram. One day before class Steve announced that he wanted to meet Amrit Desai, that he has this "desire to meet Gurudev." It just so happened that I had learned just the day prior that Amrit Desai would be coming to the studio that we practiced in. How perfect! So, of course, we were both very excited about how this opportunity came about.

Steve had been eagerly awaiting the event. Per my advice, he had selected clothing he felt appropriate to wear (after all one must look presentable when meeting a guru) and began thinking about questions to ask should the opportunity arise. Most of all he was simply excited to sit in the presence of a man who's teachings have had a profound impact on his life.

Due to miscommunication between Steve, myself, and a studio administrator, Steve missed the event. He told me later that he felt very disappointed and let down. Not only did Steve miss the opportunity to meet such an esteemed teacher, but this misunderstanding could have impacted our trusted teacher/student relationship as well. This presented an opportunity to explore attachment to expected outcomes. Not only for Steve, but for myself as well.

The day that Amrit Desai was to arrive at the yoga studio I had gone early to help prepare the space. I reserved two seats at the front of the room – one for me, one for Steve. As I worked the front desk that evening, you could feel the excitement of every guest. And I had the additional excitement of anticipating witnessing my student in the presence of my guru. Except Steve didn't come. You see, I too had expectations for that evening.

As a yoga teacher, I hope that my students get more out of their yoga practice than just exercise and relaxation (although that is very beneficial too). And of course, when teachers have a student who becomes interested in the philosophy and practical applications of yoga, we start hoping – perhaps even fanaticizing – that they will wish to go even deeper. Perhaps they will enroll in a yoga intensive program or pursue teacher training? Perhaps there will be a visit to the ashram to meet and study with our teachers? Yes, even yoga teachers are subject to setting high expectations. This experience made me realize that I had these expectations of Steve.

We both had set expectations for the evening and experienced disappointment because; whether we realized it at the time or not, we had both become attached to the idea of a specific outcome. It was because of this attachment that we both suffered from disappointment.

Though often associated with material objects, aparigraha means letting go of any fear-based attachments. We cling to possessions as a way to show a sense of personal security. We keep relationships that are not in our best interest because we are afraid of being alone. We attach to our pets because they bring such love and joy into our lives. We attach to expectations because they bring us a sense of security.

I don't think we choose to become attached to those we love. We become attached to having them in our lives. It is this attachment that causes grief, the grief turning into suffering. The more we lament over the loss, the more we live in the past memories, the more we are sad that our loved one is no longer with us. That is how suffering begins.

For me, there are still daily reminders of Griffon. A random ball found under furniture. The toy basket that I haven't yet donated. The urn that holds her ashes. If I remained attached to her, these reminders could throw me into a fit of sadness or depression, that sense of "why was she taken from me?"

But allowing myself to not be attached to her physical being, I can see these daily reminders and be okay. I am able to move at my pace to do what is appropriate with old toys, food, blankets. It's not to say that I don't get sad. In fact, I often feel tears when I think of her. But they are tears filled with beautiful memories, not tears of depression and grief. Aparigraha – non-attachment to my loved one – is allowing me to move through the process of loss and grief without getting stuck in it. Aparigraha is actually allowing me to honor Griffon by moving forward in love versus remaining stuck in the past.

Aparigraha towards a loved one who is dying is helpful to them as well. When we are with a loved one during their transition to death, they are aware of us there with them. They don't want us to be sad; they don't want us to grieve. They don't want us to suffer. So they hold on – quite consciously, perhaps fighting to do so – so that we can have more time together. When we give our loved ones permission to transition toward death and assure them that we will be okay, they can turn their attention and energy to themselves and allow the process of death to move effortlessly. Our non-attachment becomes a gift to our dying loved one because when they know we won't suffer, they are able to release their own struggle to "hold on."

In my personal example, as I lay with Griffon I could feel tension nervousness in her body. I literally told her it was okay to go; I told her I was with her and not leaving; I told her that I loved her. As I said these words I felt her whole body relax, breathing became less labored. We were able to be completely present – no past, no future. Aparigraha, non- attachment, gave us both the power and permission to be in the present experience without being limited by our past or our fears of the future.

I once studied and worked as a social worker. When it came to domestic violence, the question most frequently asked was "why did they stay?" And I have one simple answer: FEAR. The victims were often afraid of not knowing where to go, afraid to ask for help, afraid of being physically hurt or killed when they finally attempt to leave, afraid of not being able to afford to leave. For them, the fear of the unknown was greater than the fear and abuse they were experiencing every day. They became attached to the familiar, even though the familiar was abuse.

Have you ever had a married friend who could no longer stand their spouse and couldn't wait to get a divorce? Maybe it was you? And they never really were ready to make that move. "It'll be hard on the kids; I'll wait until they are a little older." "I can't afford to live on my own. I'll get a job and start saving money, and then I'll be able to leave." "I want to divorce, but I don't want to be alone." These are all excuses I have personally heard from friends and acquaintances who were contemplating divorce for one reason or another. The reason I believe each of them stayed in the relationships as long as they did (some eventually divorced, some remained married) was fear of the unknown. They were attached to the familiar.

When we are contemplating leaving a relationship – or considering any major change – we are standing at a precipice, unsure of what lies ahead. We fear the unknown because we don't know what to expect. Sometimes we become almost paralyzed by the unknown, unable to make a decision, preferring to remain with the familiar even if it's uncomfortable or painful. And this applies to any relationship: romantic, friendships, even family.

Being attached prevents us from seeing a larger picture of the situation. It prevents us from seeing the other's perspective. When we make our happiness contingent upon the relationship continuing as it always had, it prevents us from living in the present moment. We are constantly living in the past by comparing our current situation with how the relationship used to be. It also prevents the other person from being able to grow and evolve, both within the relationship and independently. When we insist upon another that they look, speak, or act in a certain manner, we prevent their natural evolution, growth and expression of self. But when we can let go of the past – whether we consider it positive or negative, good or bad – we open up the potential for infinite growth and expansion, for ourselves and those around us. This growth and expansion can then lead us toward taking appropriate action in our relationships and all aspects of life.

So, why do we become attached? It simply comes down to fear. But it really isn't so simple. When we hear that we become attached out of fear, we interpret it as a fear of loss. We are afraid to lose our things (the nice car, house, pretty clothes), afraid to lose our prestigious job, afraid our loved ones will die. So we hold it all closer and tighter out of that fear.

It is the innate nature for all our "things" to come and go. The pretty clothes will eventually wear out; the car will eventually break down and get traded in. That prestigious job? You may get another promotion or eventually retire, in essence "losing" that job. And our loved ones? Eventually our human bodies reach the end of their use and, like the car, need a trade-in. So if it is part of our natural experience that all things come and go in time, why do we try to hold onto them? Why do we fear their loss?

WE don't.

Our ego fears that as we discover our true nature we will no longer have a use for it, and therefore it will experience a type of death. Ego's purpose, generally speaking, is to help us navigate through this human experience. It is charged with keeping us safe, keeping us fed, it helps us discern what we need to do in order to experience all of being human. However, we have forgotten who we truly are. We are not the labels the ego has created for ourselves – mother, father, brother, aunt, worker, Jane, John, etc. – we are far greater than that; we are an intimate part of the greater consciousness of the Universe. Instead of recognizing this, we identify ourselves with the ego and all that it has acquired. We will explore this more as we discuss satya.

As we progress in our spiritual practices, the ego fears it will no longer be needed and will, therefore, die. When your parents pass on you are no longer a son/daughter. A piece of your ego-identity dies with them, this label of son/daughter. In one sense, this is what we mean when we say a part of us has dies when a loved one passes. Our ego suffers because it lost a part of its identity; a part of it died.

We can think of the ego as an organ. Just as the heart has the job of circulating blood, bringing nutrients to other organs and taking away their waste for elimination; the ego has a biological function. The ego is an organ of discernment, and that discernment helps this human being navigate its existence in society and keep the body safe. If I asked you to complete the sentence "I am ___" you wouldn't say "I am the heart." Or the stomach. Or the lungs. But we, essentially say "I am my ego" through the use of the labels our ego has identified with. "I am Julie, I am a writer, I am a yogi" is what I would say.

Yes, when this body has reached the end of its lifespan, all organs will cease working. The heart, the lungs, even the ego. But, as we will discover, we are not the body or the ego,; they are a part of us. And we are part of Universal Consciousness. Universal Consciousness is always present, never dies. Therefore, our true Self can never really die. We practice aparigraha so that we can end the suffering that our attachments cause. That is not to say that when a loved one dies we cannot be sad, for example. What it means is that we experience our loss, we grieve, and we move forward. We do not allow an attachment to the past.

Since Griffon's passing, I would be lying if I said I no longer felt sadness. As I write this, it has been a year since her death and there are days when I feel overwhelming sadness that she is not here. I find myself looking for her hiding in the garden; I want to call her to bed at night. But when I remember that all of creation is born out of the Universal Consciousness and that Griffon and I are part of that same Universal Consciousness, I know that we are always connected. When I remember this, I feel a sense of peace. When I forget, I feel the pain of loss, replaying that experience over and over in my mind. When I identify as Griffon's caregiver, I suffer because I can no longer fulfil that role. When I release attachment to that role, I release suffering. The same applies to you: the more you are able to release attachment to the labels you identify with, the less suffering you will experience. The less attachment to the labels, the clearer you will see your true Self.

theYA*mas*

[uh-STAY-uh]

Meaning
non-stealing

Sutra 2:37
*To one established
in non-stealing,
all wealth comes.*

Thou shall not steal. Asteya. Non-stealing. We steal due to a sense of incompleteness, a sense of not feeling whole, needing to feel secure; forgetting that we are already whole and complete. Probably the most universally recognized form of stealing is theft or larceny. Shoplifters taking items from stores without paying for them. It happens with children and teens often in response to a dare from peers, but sometimes just to see if they can get away with it. Sometimes it comes from a need to fit in, thus stealing popular clothing, music, etc. I remember my own sister stealing candy as a fairly young child. Even at that young age, when confronted she simply said she wanted to see if anyone would find out what she had done.

Some people steal because they desire an object that they cannot afford. This item becomes so attached in their mind; their desire to have it overcomes any rational thoughts. So instead of saving money towards the purchase of the item, they slip it quietly into a pocket or bag in hopes to sneak it home. Others steal so they can sell the items elsewhere. Some steal for "legitimate" needs. These are folks who, for example, cannot afford the food they need to feed their families, so they resort to stealing it.

Each scenario stems from parigraha – attachment – and the security that money, or the objects representing monetary wealth, bring to them. For whatever the reason, when we steal, it reinforces a sense of jealousy and competition, the desire to have what others have, the need to prove our worth. When we practice asteya one obvious benefit is that we are considered good citizens. But when we combine the practice of Asteya with heart and give to others, we are often gifted back even more. The more we practice asteya; we are presented with more and more opportunities to realize that we do not need to take from others. We have, or are given, all that we need.

have you ever had a day at work when you spent more time working on personal stuff than work stuff? Perhaps online shopping and looking at social media between work assignments? Now, don't worry about defending yourself – we all have days when the workload is minimal at best, or days that we are not as productive as usual. This is normal, it happens. Can you relate? What if you did this every single day and still collected the same paycheck as your consistently hard-working coworker? Did you actually work for that paycheck? Could this be considered a form of stealing? The answer to that last question is "yes." And you likely know of someone was who was terminated from their job because of it. Perhaps that person was you. When we enter an employment relationship we are essentially in a contract to perform certain tasks in exchange for financial compensation. We do work in exchange for cash.

When we are not completely honest about the tasks we completed – in quantity or quality – and we receive compensation for what we did not complete, that is a form of stealing.

For example, your job is to telephone customers who have recently made a purchase to ensure product or service satisfaction. You are not being monitored, but you are expected to contact a minimum of 50 customers each week. But you had your own appointments to schedule this, so you spent most of your time calling doctors' offices, your child's school, maybe shopped online as well. You contacted a total of five customers in between your personal calls. At the end of the week you received your regular pay. You got paid to contact 50 customers when you only contacted five – you got paid for 45 phone calls you never made. Not only could this be considered stealing the money, but you also took resources. You had use of a phone, computer, desk space, perhaps even paper goods.

We also steal from our loved ones, our family and friends. When we are with them or talking on the phone, we are taking their time and energy. Most often this is a mutual exchange. But when our needs and desires overshadow the needs and desires of our family and friends, we are being greedy.

When we are experiencing something difficult – relationship or job issues, concerns about a child, financial woes, etc. – we often turn to a close friend for support and advice. We spend the majority of that time together talking about our own issues until we find a solution, or at least until we feel better about the situation. In the case of something tragic or extreme, you will call upon that friend demanding their immediate assistance – and that friend will change all plans to be by your side in your time of need. This is essentially taking – or stealing – your friend's time. You are taking from their time with their own family, their personal time, their work or volunteer time. If your relationship is mutually supportive, then at some point in time you will "return" their time by providing the same support in their time of need.

Yet there are people who steal time from others with no intent to return the favor. We call these people self-centered and narcissistic. When with family and friends, they dominate conversation with their issues or concerns, even senseless babble, just so that attention is focused on them. Anything that happened in the world around them they believe is directly affecting them in some way. It is all about them. They are the center of their own universe, and they expect to be the center of yours as well. When you spend time in the presence of such a person, you know that you will never be able to go to that person when you need support or an ear to listen. You know that you will never have a fulfilling conversation or experience with this person. You know that your relationship with this person is not give-and-take. This person steals your time with no intent to give back.

I believe the most common, and perhaps least realized, manner of stealing is stealing from ourselves. When we had planned dinner out after work but was asked to stay longer, we cancel our plans for whatever reason motivated us to stay. We are asked to come in during our family vacation because a co-worker quit, and we say "yes." As these sorts of episodes continue we will often blame our boss or the organization – after all, they are the ones asking for our time. And to an extent, yes they bear some of that responsibility. However, we are willingly giving away our time. We are saying "yes" when we really want to say "no." We are stealing that time from ourselves.

When we excessively consume drugs or alcohol regularly, we are stealing from our health. When we regularly choose to binge-watch our favorite television series instead of exercising, we are stealing from our health. When we continually give money to a needy family member even though we are struggling financially ourselves, we are stealing from our own financial stability.

We can blame our boss for always asking us to work extra hours. We can blame our roommate for watching our favorite shows as we are heading out for the gym. We can blame our brother or sister for being irresponsible. And, although this may all be true, you are the one who is saying "yes" to it all. By saying "yes" you are stealing from your finances, your health, and your time.

how do we practice asteya when there is so much gross and subtle stealing happening all around us? Begin by observing yourself. How do you spend your time? Who do you spend it with? Are you the person who monopolizes every conversation you have; or are you the person who gives their time away? Begin to explore why you do what you do. Look for opportunities to support and give back to those who have supported and listened to you.

Where else do you steal? Do you leave work early every Friday? Have you taken a ream of copy paper from the supply room so that your child could have drawing paper at home? Then also find where you are giving away your energy, time, possessions? Where are you allowing others to steal from you?

Once you identify these you can begin to make small, incremental changes so that you are no longer stealing from others; and so that you do not allow others to steal from you. Then you begin to live a more balanced life with yourself and those around you.

the YA*mas*

braMAacharya

[bra-MAA-char-ya]

Meaning
celibacy, moderation,
returning to source

Sutra 2:38
By one established
in continence,
vigor is gained.

bramacharya may be the most misunderstood of all the yamas. Often strictly translated as celibacy, bramacharya is about maintaining moderation so as to conserve vital life energy. For those following a monastic path, this often includes sexual celibacy as bramacharya is about conserving our energy for our higher purpose.

The ancient medical system of Ayurveda also addresses the conservation of energy. There are three types of energy within the body that are functionally dependent upon each other. Ojas is a subtle energy that maintains immunity, strength, vitality and integrity to the organs and body and is the foundation for prana and tejas. Tejas is the energy of intelligence, discrimination and digestion. It gives luminosity, enthusiasm and passion. Prana is the vital life force and the intelligence that governs cellular communications, sensory perception, motor responses, and the electrical impulses of the body.

Ojas is further described as a colloidal liquid, slimy, having a honey-like taste with aromas of toasted rice, and is yellowish-white in color like ghee. This is the same description given to the substance called shukra. Shukra is a Vedic term for both seminal fluid and vaginal secretions. These secretions contain ojas. During intercourse shukra, and the associated ojas, is released from the body. When we abstain from sex, shukra builds up and is absorbed into the bodily tissues. The associated ojas is also absorbed back into the tissues. Those choosing the path of a monk were instructed on celibacy as a means to conserve ojas and vital life energy. This is where I believe the link between bramacharya and celibacy originated. And it makes sense that celibacy would be mandated among the monks because sex and other indulgences distract one from their spiritual studies.

But what about those of us who want a spiritually connected life, but also live and work in this world and want families? Moderation. Moderation in sexual activity will not deplete us of our vital life energy, or ojas. If on the other hand we became addicted to and obsessed with the pleasures of sex, we do not give our body the proper recovery time it needs to replenish the spent shukra. Over time, this can lead to illness and loss of vitality due to decreased ojas, as shukra is linked to ojas. When we practice moderation of sexual activity we maintain ojas, our health, and our vitality.

In speaking of moderation, I often think of alcohol and food. You've probably heard the medical recommendations that moderate consumption of alcohol may be beneficial. But when we indulge more often, either in quantity or frequency, we can begin to rewire our brain to desire more. Over time that one drink per week becomes one per day, that one drink per day becomes two.

Because alcohol is a depressant, it lessens our

sensitivity to energy. It could be energy in terms of thoughts, physical sensations such as pain, emotions. The less sensitive we are to these energies, the less bothered we are by them. This is a distraction that takes us away from feeling, away from being present with what is. Moderation not only prevents us from becoming inebriated, it allows us to remain fully connected to life and spirit.

Of course alcohol can become addictive, which is not really my focus here. However, I am sure you can see how one may become more engaged with the distraction and escape that alcohol can provide, even if addiction never occurs. It is this distraction that distances us from our spiritual pursuits and our authentic selves. I also see this happen frequently with food.

We have all seen it, perhaps done it ourselves. In an attempt to "eat healthier" we restrict what we allow or don't allow ourselves to eat. For this example, we decide no more sweets. No cookies. No cake. No candy. And we do okay for a while. Then one day someone brings in a box of fresh-baked cookies to your workplace. All we can smell are those cookies. All you can think of is the gooeyness of chocolate melting in a fresh from-the oven piece of heaven. Can you taste it yet? So, you figure that you have been really good and decide that you deserve one cookie – just one, it won't hurt. And you eat that cookie; and its SOOO good. Then you go back for another, and another. Perhaps you now feel like a failure on your healthy eating plan and that you have lost all self-control.

When we restrict something, we label it as good or bad. We are placing a judgement, a value, and creating separation. An apple is good, a cookie is bad. In reality neither is good or bad (in moderation); we place that value and separate them. But if I eat five apples in one sitting there could be some undesired effects on my body – bloating, feeling too full, changes in my elimination, self-judgment – just as there could be if I ate five cookies. However, if all food is just food and I consume all food moderately, both the apple and the cookie could have a place in my healthy diet.

Now, of course, I realize that there are more beneficial nutrients in the apple than are present in the cookie, but that is not the point here. When we approach our overall diet – both food and beverage – with an attitude of brahmacharya we create less stress; we create an opportunity to enjoy everything fully. Can you imagine going forward in your life never again saying "I can't have that, I'm on a diet (or something similar)," but instead moving forward simply choosing what best fuels your whole being at that time? Brahmacharya, the practice of moderation, can create more freedom and liberation, not a sense of restriction, in our lives.

antoher area we can benefit from bringing more moderation into our lives is in our speech. Using less words to say what we need to say, using a calm voice. Although this may be pleasing to the person receiving our message, it's more about conserving our personal energy.

On a day-to-day basis, we have all known someone who dominates all conversations, seemingly to never quiet. Or a person who talks very loudly. Yes, it can be tiring for the person listening, but imagine, if you can, that it's you. Imagine that you are always talking, talking, talking… seemingly never stopping to take a breath. How tiring that must feel? Or imagine talking super loud all the time. Wouldn't your throat and vocal cords hurt after time? Imagine how tiring it must be for these individuals, and imagine how much energy that takes from other functions in their life.

When we are moderate in our speech we conserve energy in our body, much the same as when we are moderate in sexual activity. When we limit the amount of words we use, we don't need to speak for as long. When we slow the pace of our speech, we feel more relaxed in speaking. When we talk at a moderate pace others often better understand what we say because they can actually hear everything we are saying. When we speak in softer tones we preserve the health of our voice. It also takes less effort to produce sound versus when we speak loudly or yell.

although we can select many more examples of how to practice – or not practice – moderation in our life, it is my hope that you can see how moderation conserves your energy. "The reason for practicing brahmacharya is not to create an idealistic principle that leads to guilt and self-rejection, but to cultivate and facilitate the process that leads to Self-discovery… [It] means not indulging in sensuality, thoughts or emotions that drain your vital life force, the powerful vehicle for Self-discovery and Self-realization" (Desai p.54). When we conserve our energy we are able to think clearer and with greater discernment.

When we overly indulge our senses, we become attached to the feeling it gives us. Whether we are indulging in sex, drugs, alcohol, food, shopping; if it is giving us a type of "high" as we are partaking in the activity, we are more likely to indulge in that behavior more and more frequently. We will be anxiously waiting the next time we get to partake in that activity. Taking part in the activity, and awaiting the next time we get to take part, depletes our vital energy.

The desire for our next "hit," that next opportunity to indulge ourselves, creates a level of suffering. First because we are suffering for not having what we want when we want it. Ultimately we suffer because we are distracting ourselves from our higher purpose, our higher Self.

Now I caution you from becoming overly enthusiastic about practicing brahmacharya. One of my teachers would say to practice moderation in all things, even moderation with moderation itself. What do I mean by this? Have you ever seen a person who was very diligent in their personal regimens? Someone who was very deliberate in only eating the proper recommended portion sizes each meal?

A person who was so deliberate in exercising exactly five days per week for no less than 30 minutes per day (for 150 minutes total, as medically recommended)? A person so deliberately attached to their chosen form of moderation that it literally pains them if they cannot practice this strict form of moderation? In this case, the act of practicing moderation is what the person desires, becoming attached to moderation and suffering because of that attachment.

So become aware of where you spend your personal energy. Notice the things you enjoy, and observe how you would feel if they were suddenly no longer available to you. If you notice a sense of desire and attachment, perhaps begin to not indulge in that activity as often. As examples, having sex three times a week versus every day; eating chocolate only after dinner compared to after every meal; having only one glass of wine with dinner versus three. Additionally, observe where you are being over-diligent in the practice of moderation. Can you allow yourself some freedom and less self-regulation around that?

By conserving our physical energy, we preserve that energy for our spiritual pursuits. We have more energy to explore and discover our true nature. After all, the literal translation of brahmacharya is "to move toward Brahman [God]" (Desai 53). As we move toward this realization of Self we find that we are naturally able to fully enjoy all sensual pleasures without over- or under-indulging.

the YA*mas*

[a-HIM-sah]

Meaning
non-violence, non-harming

Sutra 2:35
*In the presence
of one firmly estsblished
in non-violence,
all hostilities cease.*

ahimsa is traditionally the first yama taught to yogis. It is said that when one is firmly established in ahimsa, all other disciplines naturally fall into place. Ahimsa, or non-harming, truly is the heart of a yogic practice, as well as the heart of every other spiritual practice. Yet, it can also be one of the hardest to master.

When the ancient yogis and sages introduced these teachings, the first concept they tried to share was that unconditional love is always present. But it is difficult for the human mind to conceptualize and fully understand unconditional love. Unconditional love is the caring or loving thoughts and attention we give to ourselves and others with absolutely no stipulations, terms or conditions, or expectations of return. Unconditional love is to be expressed toward all beings at all times regardless of the situations.

It is easy to love our family. Even if we are mad at them, we generally wish them well and care for them deeply. We show love to our pets who naturally love us unconditionally as well. Imagine for a moment the love you feel for your child (or your pet or a child you are close to if you are not a parent). Sometimes your child is an absolute angel; sometimes they act more like a demon, testing every last bit of your patience. Even though you may be upset toward your child at times, you still love them equally every day, every moment – regardless of what happens. That is unconditional love.

But to truly express unconditional love you must also extend that same love and care to those who appear underserving, those who may have done wrong in society. The person who willingly flies a plane into a building with the intent of killing hundreds of people should also receive your love. Because love is unconditional it does not matter if a person is your angelic child, your loving partner, a stranger on the street, or a terrorist; all beings should be looked upon with love.

This is a very difficult concept for our human minds to contemplate. "How can I show love to someone, such as a terrorist, who only wants to hurt people?" The ancient yogis understood this, so instead of teaching that we should show love toward every being, they taught us to do no harm to others.

We are taught through ahimsa to not bring harm or suffering to any being – person, animal or insect. If someone does something bad or wrong to us, we do not retaliate by causing them harm in return. Even if a person commits an act of extreme violence, we do not wish harm to be caused to them. We can be angry at the situation, but we do not wish for them to be hurt in any way. If we wish harmful things to happen to the terrorist we are not acting from a place of love for all existence. Additionally, wishing harm to someone who caused harm is simply perpetuating the cycle of violence, even if you do not physically act on those thoughts. When we approach people and situations with the attitude of not causing harm, we give those around us permission to do the same.

It is through this practice of non-harming that we begin to recognize that all living beings are divine. Meaning that all beings, including ourselves, come from god. So we begin to treat others with reverence. One of the things that make ahimsa so difficult to practice fully is that we often forget ourselves. Our modern society trains us to be so hard on ourselves in the quest for success. We, as a society, speak so violently of ourselves and to ourselves. We hardly treat ourselves with respect, let alone with love.

Ahimsa is the practice of Unconditional Love. The Bible states that we should love our neighbor as we love ourselves. But what if we don't treat ourselves with love? If we treat ourselves with hate and violent thoughts, how are we likely to treat our neighbors? Cause no harm to any human, animal or creature in your thoughts or deeds, including one's self.

How many times have you found yourself saying "that was so stupid, I can't believe I did that?" Or "that was so dumb of me?" Or perhaps it sounds more like "I'm such an asshole?" Such language is hurtful to others, and it's hurtful to us. The more we hear it, the more we believe it. The more we believe it the more willing we are to accept such talk, whether from ourselves or from others. It becomes normal. The more harm we speak towards ourselves the more distance we place between ourselves and love; the more distant from love, the more distant from god.

As we begin to see the world through the lens of ahimsa, all interactions – whether with others or our own self-talk – becomes an opportunity to not cause harm or suffering. "Ahimsa is the sate that exists when all violence in the heart and mind have subsided. It is not something we have to acquire; it is always present and only needs to be uncovered. When one practices ahimsa, or nonviolence, one refrains from causing distress – in thought, word or deed – to any living creature, including oneself" (Desai 51). It is through this act of choosing not to cause harm that the true understanding of unconditional love is revealed.

I feel it would be irresponsible of me not to mention ahimsa toward our environment. For decades – centuries, really – humans have caused harm to the natural environment of the earth. We are destroying forests. We are polluting the air with chemicals, the land with trash. Several species have become extinct with many, many more soon to follow. Even our own food supplies are tainted with harmful chemicals.

We, as a collective whole, are clearly not practicing ahimsa towards our planet. There are simple ways that we all can begin to be less violent to the natural world around us. If you do not already recycle, begin. Most municipalities offer curb-side recycle pick-ups as part of their rubbish removal programs. Perhaps your city or town has a recycling program but your apartment complex does not provide receptacles for recycling pick-up (as is the case for a friend of mine), then consider bringing your recycling items to a family member or friend to add to their pick-up bins. The yoga studio I teach at does not have recycling receptacles for the building, so the staff members take turns bringing the items for recycling home to our personal bins for municipal pick-up.

We can choose organic over conventional foods. Designated organic foods are limited in what types and quantities of chemical fertilizers and pest control they are able to use. And the more organic foods that are purchased, the more that will become available (incidentally, that will also make them less expensive). After all, organic food is natural; and organic and biodynamic farming practices protect and give back nutrients to our farmland.

Walk, bike, or take public transit to work. Walking or bicycling is an excellent option as it is kind to both the earth and our bodies – no toxic emissions and our body gets exercise. Utilize public transportation as it reduces the number of vehicles on the road. And if you live in an area where public transit is near non-existent and work is too far to bike, then consider an electric or hybrid vehicle as they produce low-to-zero emissions into the environment.

If you have a yard or balcony plant flowers that are beneficial to bees. Bees are essential to our food supply (and the food supply of most land-dwelling creatures) as they pollinate plants; pollination is how plants reproduce and generate the parts that we consume. By providing flowers for bees to enjoy, you are providing them with food and helping to ensure their survival. Plus, I find them entertaining to watch. If you are adventurous and have the space, consider establishing your own hive as a beekeeper.

Consider your immediate surroundings, such as home or office. Choosing natural cleaners and air fresheners helps to keep your immediate surroundings toxin-free, but also eliminates a portion of toxins released into the environment as a whole. I find most natural air fresheners (be it in the forms of candles, oils, or incense) to have a much cleaner scent. Natural cleaners, likewise, have a cleaner aroma and I find them to be less harsh on my lungs.

If you have some of the same tendencies as I do, then you may be stuck wondering how you are going to ever not wish harm toward murderers and other evil doers. Stop worrying; it will come with practice. I have a simple exercise that you can do over time to encourage the practice of ahimsa.

To begin, start easy. Think about your loved ones – family and close friends. It is easy to think kind, loving thoughts towards them. Observe your thoughts as you interact with your loved ones each day. Inevitably there will be an incident that occurs that leaves you frustrated or angry with your loved one. When this happens observe your thoughts, notice the words you choose. Don't be surprised if your initial reactions are full of harsh words or even hatred. Just notice your tendencies, and remember that just because you have these reactions does not mean you no longer care for your loved ones.

The next step is to practice changing your reactions. If during an argument you spoke harmful words, practice pausing before speaking. Ask yourself if the words you are about to speak could be harmful. If the answer is "yes" either change the words or choose not to speak at all. Then observe your thoughts about your loved one both during the incident and following the incident. Notice the thoughts you have about your loved one; and if they contain anger or hate begin to change those thoughts to something more neutral. Moving from "I can't believe how stupid my child was" to something along the lines of "I can't believe my child made such a poor decision" is moving in the right direction.

When you feel you have gained skill in practicing ahimsa toward loved ones, begin the same process towards someone you feel more neutral towards. This could be a coworker, a neighbor, someone from your gym. Observe your thoughts and language during interactions with this person. How do you address this person? What are your thoughts when they mess up a project at work? Thoughts about what you consider to be "tacky" lawn ornaments at your neighbor's house? Observe the tone of your language and thoughts, moving from potentially hurtful toward more neutral language.

Then repeat this process with someone who hurt you physically or emotionally in the past, someone you have held deep resentment towards. Observe the thoughts and feelings that arose just from reading this instruction. This one will take some time to work with, be patient but consistent. Revisit thinking about this person and work toward moving your thoughts away from wishing them harm in return for what they did to you, and move from calling them rude or hurtful names toward more neutral words and thoughts.

You can use this process with strangers who have committed some horrible crime. Examples include child molesters, rapists, murderers, terrorists. You could be watching a news report on a particular incident and observe your thoughts and reactions, keeping in mind that you can still experience a sense of anger over the act that was committed but begin to separate the person from the event. Move thoughts about the person from hateful toward neutral.

Lastly, turn this exercise toward yourself. By now you are well-practiced and have the skill. Observe how you think about and refer to yourself. Observe how you refer to yourself when speaking with others. Begin to move from harmful towards neutral thoughts and words.

Finally, observe how this whole process has made you feel. Notice how it feels to not harbor hate and anger towards others. Notice that there is a sense of peace and stillness that is becoming more and more present. This stillness is love. It is the always present, all-encompassing ability to see all beings, regardless of the acts or deeds they perform, in the same unconditional light of ahimsa.

the YAmas

[sut-YAH]

Meaning
truth

Sutra 2:36
To one established in truthfulness, actions and their results become subservient.

truth. A simple concept on the surface, but its deeper meanings really point to the basic premise that underlies all the yamas. I am not aware of any religion that does not place value upon telling the truth. We are taught that honesty is one of the highest virtues; a person that is honest receives the highest respect. And yet so many people tell lies.

Those "little white lies" you sometimes tell are still lies. Even though they seem harmless or are out of good intentions, you're still not being truthful. An excited friend asks you if you like their new shirt or tie and you say "yes" because you know they really like it, but you honestly think it's very ugly or unflattering. Even though you avoided hurting your friend's feelings, you were not truthful.

I have found that people tell lies for two reasons: to avoid hurting others or fear. When we fear the consequences of telling the truth it becomes very easy to lie. As children we may lie about who broke mom's favorite vase because we were afraid of what our punishment would be. As we get older it may be lies about taking something (stealing), lies about where we are going. At work, we may lie about our level of involvement in an unsuccessful project because we fear being demoted or losing our job.

Telling lies can become exhausting. Once we tell a lie we need to continue to support that story with more lies so that no one discovers the truth. Honesty, on the other hand, conserves our energy and can decrease our fears. When we approach each other with honesty we no longer fear being "discovered."

Satya is more than being truthful in thoughts and actions. Satya is the ultimate truth that all existence is connected. All of existence is connected and is not separate. Living in this knowledge is living in Satya.

Scientifically speaking, we can reduce everything down to atoms and empty space. Things that we perceive as being solid – tables, walls, wood, iron – actually contain more empty space that matter. They are simply condensed more than, say, air. This concept applies to objects, creatures, galaxies. Even you and your physical body is just a bunch of atoms and empty space condensed to the point of appearing to take a distinct form. Not only this, but everything is made from the same atoms; they are just arranged together in different ways. This means quite literally that we are, at our core, no different than any person, creature, or thing. We are truly made of the same exact molecules.

Of course, something has to orchestrate this coming together of atoms, molecules and space. Some people call it god, universe; for our purposes here I am calling it Universal Consciousness. Universal Consciousness is made up of the same atoms and space as the things it creates. To give an illustration of how this works, imagine an ocean. And within that ocean waves emerge, then return to the ocean. The waves appear distinct, but they are not separate from the ocean. You cannot go to the beach, pick up a wave and take it home with you. However, you can observe this distinct form that you call a wave rise up from the ocean and return to the ocean. The waves are simply condensed ocean. In this analogy, the ocean represents Universal Consciousness and the waves are all the things created within it and by it. Things become condensed parts of Universal Consciousness (the ocean) to the point of seeming solid and separate (the wave), then they return to Universal Consciousness when their purpose is done. Humans arise out of this ocean of Universal Consciousness at birth, we return to the ocean of Universal Consciousness when we die, just as the wave arises out of the water only to return to the water.

If you are following this logic, you may begin to see that you were created by, from and within Universal Consciousness. This means that you are Universal Consciousness. You are the Universe, you are divine, you are god.

There is a mantra, or prayer, known through the yogic and spiritual communities as the Asatoma mantra. In it we ask to be lead from the "unreal to the real," or, we could say, from untruth to truth. Seeking truth is active. It requires study, testing, observation, assessment, and application of new knowledge gained. It requires us to repeat this process continuously. Seeking truth is swadhyaya. Swadhyaya is self-study so that we may re-discover and know our true nature.

I have heard it said that dishonesty helps us to survive. The 'little white lies,' perjury on the witness stand, the denial of our actions all serve the purpose of protecting ourselves – or others – in some way. Likewise our ego lies to us. It tells us that we are this body, this personality that inhabits the body, and that we are all the roles this personality plays. My ego tells me I am "Julie," yoga teacher, wife, sister, etc. My ego wants me to forget my inherent connection to the Universe, to god. It wants me to forget that I AM Universal Consciousness. The ego wants us to forget the truth of our nature so that it may continue to survive. The ego fears it will become useless, therefore leading to its death. So the ego's dishonesty is a survival mechanism. But when we merely survive without knowledge of Truth we suffer. Survival is suffering.

I see this in so many circumstances, mundane and spiritual. We tell a lie to minimize another's pain. Your spouse asks how they look in a new outfit; you think it's horrible, but tell them they look great because you do not want to hurt their feelings. At lunch with their best friend, the friend tells them that the outfit does not look good on them. Your spouse suddenly feels hurt from your innocent lie, you feel pain when confronted. Your dishonesty was intended to keep your spouse happy (type of survival) but you both ended upset (suffering).

The family pet dies and you dispose of it properly.

When your young child comes home and asks for their pet you say it got out of the house and ran away – I know so many people who have done something like this. So the child starts looking for their beloved pet: searching the yard and neighborhood, putting up posters, asking people if they have seen their pet. The child is sad and suffering that they don't know where their pet has gone; you are suffering watching the pain your child is in.

Likewise our ego is dishonest. It tells us how we should view ourselves and the world. The ego tells us we are this body and all that is contained within it. The ego does this for its own survival. So we have views and opinions of ourselves and the world; opinions of what we should do and how we should do it. We have ideas of how the world should be. And there is a disconnect from what we experience through our ego and the world; this disconnect causes suffering in the forms of stress, anger, depression. It is when we remember our oneness with all of it that the stress, depression, and anger begin to subside.

When we are asked to complete the sentence "I am ___" we come up with all sorts of ways to fill in that blank. Ego identifies with the descriptors. But they are only descriptions of "I," not the "I" itself. They are the things that describe you; they are not you. This 'remembering' is what many refer to as an 'awakening." We are awakening to the truth of our nature, the truth of ourselves. This truth is our personal truth of who we are, truth of how the world is. It is this experience that shows me proof of my intimate connection to god, to Universal Consciousness. When you remember – awaken to truth – it is your proof of who you are. It is your personal truth.

So continue speaking truth. Continue seeking truth. Continue to study and look deep. Ask if what you see, think, believe is true. Try to see the ocean within the wave, the Universal Consciousness within all people and creatures. It takes time and patience, but we eventually begin to understand – and feel – how truly interconnected we all are.

the niYAmas

[knee-YAH-maas]
Sutra 2:32

> Niyama consists of
> purity, contentment, accepting
> but not causing pain, study of scriptural books
> and worship of God (self-surrender).

the niYAmas

santosha

[san-TOE-shah]

Meaning
contentment

Sutra 2:42
*By contentment,
supreme joy is gained.*

repeat this phrase to yourself: I am completely at peace with myself as I am and the world as it is.

In my yoga tradition we often state this phrase during guided meditations, and even during regular asana (physical postures) classes. This statement is an affirmation that no matter what is happening in the world around me – and, perhaps more importantly, no matter what is happening within me – we can always find a sense of stillness. Always.

This peace and stillness is Santosha, or contentment.

Contentment can describe a person's level of satisfaction. It can also be defined as "to limit (oneself) in requirements, desires or actions" (Merriam-Webster). To put a yogic spin on this definition we could say that by choosing to limit our desires (brahmacharya), our possessions and our actions (ahimsa) we develop less attachment (aparigraha) and foster the growth of contentment (Santosha). Santosha grows from not desiring something to be different than it is. This is not to say that one cannot work toward goals or toward improving their lives. Quite contrary, we should work toward improving our lives and the lives of others. If there is a need for higher education, a better paying job, a new car, or to purchase a house then go for it. But remember to remain contented in the present moment even as you embark on these endeavors.

A key to contentment is not choosing something is better or worse than what you already have. As an example, it's okay to want a newer car. There are practical reasons to support this: safety, reliability, more efficient, less likely to break down, repairs are less costly. But when we start to call a new car "better" and our current car "bad" we create a desire for the newer car and disdain for our current one. When we do this, two things happen. First, we become unhappy with our current situation. Second, we make our happiness contingent upon something or someone outside ourselves. In this case, we won't feel happy until we have a new car.

Amrit Desai states that santosha "is the ability to tolerate and digest all the opposing experiences of duality with the equanimity of the ocean. Even though all rivers flood into the ocean, it remains unperturbed, allowing all waters… to enter its vastness. Similarly, the yogi lives in the world, yet remains content, despite the ebbs and flows of life" (Desai 57). We are the ocean: vast, open, spacious Universal Consciousness. This Universal Consciousness does not have preferences or desires for things to be other than they are at any given moment. All experiences are equally welcomed, equally experienced. It is our individual ego-self that judges, that wants experiences to be different out of fear and the need to protect the ego-self. Dr. David

Frawley states contentment "means finding happiness inside ourselves rather than in outer involvement. As long as we are discontented and distracted, we will not have the peace and consistency to look within. Yoga is not a movement of the disturbed mind seeking entertainment, but a movement of the calm mind seeking inner truth. We should cultivate contentment by cultivating inner sources of creativity and awareness" (Frawley 267-268).

    For me, practicing being grateful has brought me closer to contentment. Grateful is defined as "appreciative of benefits received" or "pleasing by reason of comfort supplied or discomfort alleviated" (Miriam-Webster). By these definitions we may presume that we can only be grateful for the "good" things in our lives. We should certainly be grateful for all the blessings in our lives, but we should also cultivate gratitude toward the "bad" things as well. Why? By the very definition of grateful there are benefits to what we perceive as bad things happening. It could be a lesson learned from a mistake made, we don't get something we wanted but later something better comes along. Using the new car example, I see a car I like and make arrangements to trade my old vehicle; my loan application is not approved and I cannot purchase the car. I may feel angry or disappointed at the time, but fast forward a couple weeks. There is another dealer with a fantastic sale on the same car model I was previously looking at, someone offers to purchase my old vehicle at a higher price than the original trade offer, and I have no problems securing a loan. How many times has something like this happened to you or someone you know? And we are always so grateful for the streak of luck. But we should also be grateful for not getting that first car – because the situation would have been much different should we have purchased that first vehicle.

If course we experience disappointment, anger, and even grief when something "bad" happens. And it is absolutely appropriate to feel those emotions at the time. But when things settle, look back and ask yourself "Is there a lesson? What can I be grateful for in this situation?" so that you can practice cultivating gratitude and thankfulness with everything equally. The more that we practice being grateful for everything – good and bad, without labeling – the more things to be grateful for will come into our lives. The more we practice, the easier it becomes so that, eventually, we are effortlessly grateful for everything all the time. That is contentment to me.

Look back at the Introduction and my story about Griffon. Her death was devastating to me, just as the death of any loved one would be. When I begin to feel sad about this loss, I remember all the joy and I am grateful for our time together. I am also grateful to have been able to care for her medically, even though it was painful for both of us at times. And I am also grateful for the lessons she taught me at her death. Without those lessons this book would never have been conceived of, let alone written. There is always something to be grateful for, we just have to practice looking for it.

A second component to remember is that contentment can only be cultivated from within us. No person, no object, no pet can make us happy. We might say "my spouse makes me happy" but what is really happening is that they are bringing out the happiness that is already inside us; they help you to see it. When we get that new car we say we are happy because of the new car. In reality we had happiness within us; we just did not allow ourselves to feel happy without the new car.

Satchidananda states "Contentment means just to be as we are without going to outside things for our happiness…Contentment means neither to like nor dislike" (Satchidananda 146). Without judgement or labels, without for or against, we practice gratitude for all experiences in our life, cultivating this attitude of gratitude. This attitude of gratitude brings forth the contentment that resides naturally within us so that we can see it. And when we can see and recognize it, we can nurture it. We nurture contentment so that we can live in greater alignment with santosha.

Contentment is beyond simple gratitude. It is about bringing us fully present to the here and now – the only place that you or I exist.

We spend so much of our energy being anxious over what the future holds. We ponder over what will happen in regards to jobs, finances, relationships, even the state of world affairs. These are things that are off in some future time, a future time that does not yet exist. And at the same time we ruminate over things that happened in the past. It could have been ten years ago, one year ago, a day ago, or even just an hour ago but we replay the events in our mind as if they were happening in real-time. But those memories are not actually happening, they are no longer real. When we spend our time thinking about times-gone-by or worrying about an unknown future we are never fully present in the now.

Imagine standing along a gently flowing river. You dip your toes into the water and pull them out quickly. You decide to step back into the river. Are you standing in the same water as you did when you first dipped your toes in? No; although it may look the same, that water has already flowed downstream. What is waiting upstream in the future eventually flows into the present moment, but it quickly floats further downstream and into the past. You can never be in that moment again. Until we are able to find contentment in the present moment – the now – we will always be searching for it elsewhere.

Now, planning for future events does have its place in our modern society. You make appointments with your doctor, for example, and it's helpful to remember those dates and plan accordingly – such as scheduling time out of work. It is helpful to have goals to reach towards, using them as guideposts that you are on track. Likewise, remembering certain things that have occurred in the past may have a practical purpose. If as a child you had placed your hand on a hot stove it would probably be beneficial to remember this so that it does not happen again. A former friend had abused your trust; it may be helpful to remember that incident so that you do not place your trust in them in the future. Memory and planning are useful, and needed, in our modern society. It is when we dwell on them that we lose contentment.

    Contentment can only happen when we are fully present in the here and now. Each moment. Each now.

    To help cultivate this ability there is an exercise I do with my yoga students. From my own experience I know that my mind can get very busy worrying that I won't be able to do a particular pose or that I will aggravate and injury. Or I find myself wondering what the teacher will have us do next. Also from my experience, I know that my students are no different. So I will lead them into poses that I know will bring up mental chatter for them. It might be a pose that a student really dislikes, we may hold a pose for a longer period of time, or perhaps I begin to lead them into a pose that they fear may aggravate an injury of their own (of course, I lead something modified and safe so they do not get hurt). As we are moving into and holding a pose I ask my students to observe their thoughts: to watch their thoughts like clouds in the sky. Thoughts float in, thoughts float out. What they often think I am doing is helping them stay calm and focused – and, yes, this is happening – but I am also showing them that they can stay present despite all the thoughts and ideas coming and going.

It takes practice, though. We are so accustomed to dwelling in the past and being anxious about the future that we do not know – or, more accurately, we don't remember – how to be fully present in the now moment. And I am no exception. We all need to practice this, every day and every moment.

Contentment is neither liking nor disliking, it is not wanting anything to be different than it is. It is not needing to seek happiness in things or people; we can find happiness in ourselves moment to moment. The feeling of stillness, peace, the lack of anxiety or fear that one experiences does not compare to anything else. Those are words that describe what it is like to be truly present. Those are words that describe the feeling of being content.

the niYAmas

SAUCHA

[saw-CHA]

Meaning
purity, cleanliness, holiness, sacredness

Sutra 2:40-41

By purification arises disgust for one's own body and for contact with others. Moreover, one gains purity of sattva, cheerfulness of mind, one-pointedness, mastery over the senses, and fitness for self-realization.

Cleanliness and purification have two components, in the yogic sense: physical and internal/mental. Both of these have practical and spiritual implications. Physical cleanliness begins with our physical body. We bathe regularly to clear dirt, sweat, and other unpleasant things from our body. We wear clean clothing that is appropriate for our environment. For example, we would wear warm jackets and sweaters in cold winters, shorts and tee shirts in the hot summer. We eat a proper, nutritious diet; one that nourishes our body and provides key nutrients. We don't over- or under-eat; we apply brahmacharya in that we do not overindulge, but we also do not over restrict ourselves. We exercise to keep our body physically fit.

Physical cleanliness includes our immediate surroundings. Our bedrooms, living and work spaces. We keep them clean, neat, and organized. We avoid clutter and hoarding. Amrit Desai includes what we do for work as well how we put the yamas and niyamas into practice as aspects of saucha.

There are a group of Buddhist ideals that direct a practitioner toward proper behaviors. The concept of right livelihood (Snelling 50-51) is centered on the practice of ahimsa. Whatever we do for work should cause no harm to ourselves or others at minimum, and if possible it should do well for others in the world. Additionally, the Buddhist concept of right effort, to me, summarizes the idea of proper practice of all the yamas and niyamas. We do not want to practice too hard or with too little effort. Snelling writes "proper effort is not the effort to make something particular happen. It is the effort to be aware and awake in each moment… the effort to make each activity of our day meditation" (Snelling 50). It is with this mindset that we begin to move from purity of body and physical surrounding to purity of mind.

The essence of saucha is that we must first understand and purify our body, and then we can begin to purify our soul (Satchidandanda 145). This is the internal purification of thoughts, emotions and habits. By observing our thoughts we can begin to discern whether they serve our greater good or whether they no longer benefit us. Using the filter of ahimsa we can sort out the thoughts, emotions and habits that are harmful to ourselves and others. It is not to label them as either good or bad, but simply whether they support us on our spiritual path or not.

In my yoga tradition, we utilize our asana practice to purify us internally by first purifying our bodies. By coming to the yoga mat and moving through various postures we purify our physical body by releasing toxins through movement and sweat. We begin to purify our mind as we observe thoughts, feelings, physical sensations, and our automatic responses to those thoughts, feelings, and sensations as they arise during our asana practice. We will look more deeply into this as we discuss tapas.

"…our intention is to heal our body, clear our mind and purify our heart, and bring them into alignment with our highest potential… Saucha happens when we are the witness. As we cease to nourish our thoughts by identifying with them, fighting them, denying them or suppressing them, they die of starvation. We are left with the awareness of our inherent innocence, purity and oneness with the Source" (Desai 57). By purifying the body and mind, we clear away all that blocks our view of the truth, or satya, of our divine nature.

how do we purify body and mind? Scripture says through the yogic practices. The practice of yoga asana and meditation create a steadiness of mind. This does not mean we are void of thoughts, but that our mind does not waiver in the presence of new or multiple thoughts. Imagine an excited child whose attention keeps moving from one thing to another. "Look there! What's that over there? A squirrel! Oh, is that a puppy…" Their mind is not steady. The same is for us as we are bombarded by new thoughts, new information coming to us through our senses. An unsteady mind will bounce from thought to think just like the excited child. A steady mind will notice the new thoughts but will stay concentrated on the task at hand rather than become distracted by the new information.

Meditation is how we practice steadiness of mind. Many get discouraged with meditation because they think their minds should become empty when they meditate. In reality meditation is practicing being steady despite the multitude of thoughts. It is the practice of allowing thoughts to come into awareness, but letting them go just as easily.

We support our meditation and yoga practices in the way we care for our body. We eat nourishing foods, we bathe regularly, we keep our homes clean, and we keep our body active. By keeping our body and surroundings pure (clean), our mind is reminded of and supported in efforts towards steadiness (purity of mind).

When our mind is steady, or pure, we act according to what is appropriate (right action) without being distracted by thoughts: what would people think, is this right, should I do this instead, etc. It is a process and takes practice, but does get easier with time. The purer – or steadier – our mind becomes, the closer we come to understanding Truth.

the niYAmas

taPAS

[ta-PAAS]

Meaning
spiritual heat

Sutra 2:43
*By austerity,
impurities of body
and senses are destroyed
and occult powers gained.*

tapas, translating literally as "to burn, is the fire – or passion – of discipline. It is the discipline to follow our exercise regimens; the discipline to eat a healthful diet; the discipline to follow our spiritual practices.

When we are exercising we can feel the heat build within our body. In fact, the beginning of most exercise programs include a series of "warm ups" specifically designed to warm the body. This makes our joints and muscles less stiff and prepares them for more rigorous movement. As we continue with our exercise we may begin to sweat due to the heat building within our body. This heat helps to "burn" excess fat and toxins from our body. A gentle yoga class will even begin with a simple movements to begin to wake up – and warm up – the body. Even yogic breath work practices (pranayama) can create heat within the body.

True tapas come from our discipline to practice. This occurs on many levels from the physical to mental, from the mundane to spiritual. When we approach our physical practices – be it yoga, running, lifting weights, etc. – with passion and determination we encourage the heat of tapas. When we first embark on a new fitness routine it can be difficult. It may be difficult to lift weights because we lack the strength. Running may be difficult because we lack endurance. Yoga is difficult because we feel we lack the flexibility necessary to move easily in and out of postures. These difficulties have the power to make us want to quit. But when we are able to move past these resistances and continue to perform our exercise regularly, we notice our body begins to feel physically lighter, clearer. We enjoy this feeling, so we want to exercise more. This is tapas burning in our body and fueling our discipline.

Tapas can show up in cleaning our home and doing laundry. To be honest, the day-to-day cleaning bores me. But I do find the proverbial spring cleaning - the deep clean that takes you into the nooks and crannies of your home – to be much more satisfying. Once I start it often takes several days (or weeks) to complete, but as I see small areas of my home transform I become inspired to bring that super-clean transformation to other rooms. For others, the daily quick clean brings the same inspiration. This is tapas, the inspirational fire. Some find this in yardwork, dishwashing, laundry. I love laundry! I enjoy folding with meticulous care. Folding laundry becomes almost meditative for me. This deep focus, that too is tapas.

Tapas cultivated in the mundane.

The discipline of tapas shows up in anything we are passionate about and undertake at full force. Tapas is the inspiration that keeps us going even when – especially when – we cannot see the finish line.

In terms of yoga practice, however, tapas is not just about getting on your mat and performing postures every day. Tapas is part of the process of stripping away that which no longer serves us so that we may re-discover our True Selves.

Tapas can be understood as the "burning of unconscious activities; adopting the specific discipline of yoga with the intention to burn all karma. When it burns it creates heat, irritation, fear, resistance, self-defense, desire to blame" (Desai 120). Desai further describes the role of karma as the "experience of the past, returning again and again in the present, giving us new opportunities to encounter it consciously and resolve it. The action we perform is karma and the reaction to the action that we experience is the result of karma" (Desai 116). Swami Satchidananda simply defined karma as "action and reaction" (Satchidananda 241). When we are on the yoga mat, we deliberately put ourselves into positions that allow us to experiences those unresolved experiences in the present so that it can become resolved. This can show up in many forms. A basic example I give in my yoga classes is to think about your knees. I use the knees because most of us have injured them at one point or another, or we have chronic issues with them. So, think about a past or current knee condition. I then imagine I ask you to move into a yoga pose (or other form of exercise) that you believe will put excess strain, or cause further injury, to your knee. A whole conversation starts in your mind over the anticipated pain you will experience before even going into the pose. This is karma; specifically the experience of a past injury returning in the present moment. Our initial re-action is an automatic response to avoid pain without testing it out. This re-action will only perpetuate this experience-memory returning again and again; and anything that invokes a similar feeling will receive the same response as well. But if we change our automatic reaction to something else that is appropriate – in this case, perhaps we slowly ease into the yoga pose to experiment whether pain arises or not – we begin to re-wire our automatic response to this experience-memory. It is in that gap between the arising of our automatic thoughts and choosing another action that tapas, the burning, occurs.

Tapas and the transformation it brings, arises in the gap between impact (first awareness of the experience-memory) and action. Do we continue in the unconscious patterns we always have, or do we make a conscious decision to act differently?

Clearly tapas plays a vital role in motivating and transforming our lives in the mundane, everyday sense. But yoga is truly about our spiritual development and, likewise, tapas plays a vital role here. Tapas is the burning of years – even lifetimes – of karma and identification with the self-image. Even enlightened beings, who create new karma in their present lives, "have to go through their prārabdha karma, which is the past karma attached to this life before we are born. This is why some enlightened masters experience physical suffering, such as cancer, diabetes and other illnesses" (Lad, Vol 2, 195). Tapas clears the path toward re-discovering our True nature, our True Selves. But only if we choose to walk that path.

A dear friend and mentor once said "the spiritual path is not for the faint of heart." It takes strength, discipline and willpower to continue on the path as things get difficult. Yes tapas is the fire of discipline and dedication; but it is also the fire that will destroy all that you have identified with up until now. It is the burning away of all the false identifications that hide your True identity (Desai 60).

According to Ayurveda, we digest not just food, but also thoughts and emotions. Vasant Lad explains "emotion is a reaction, a type of food for the mind. Thought is a response of memory, but every sensation, thought, feeling and emotion must be digested, absorbed and assimilated in order to yield right understanding" (Lad, Vol 2 193). The digestive fire (agni) is the fire of transformation, or perhaps could be understood as another form of tapas. As tapas ignites it fans agni so it is strong. We begin to more fully digest and transform our food and more fully process deep emotions. As this agni-fire works we may feel a sense of heat build within our body. This can occur during our yoga practice or any time throughout the day. We may feel feverish and ill due to the heat and elimination of ama (toxins) from the body. These sensations are normal. Take care to rest as needed.

You may also experience fear and resistance. Fear has a practical function: to maintain what you identify with for survival of the ego. We become afraid of what we see or have experienced so far, so we begin to resist the process. "The dying process of the self-image engages the ego in the same instinctive [survival] reactions it uses to protect itself from threats to physical survival, health and well-being. This tapas is the alchemy where the unconscious is turned into consciousness and the preprogrammed self-image is transformed into the Self' (Desai 61). The ego-self fears its own demise and does all it can to ensure its survival.

For one who is genuinely seeking truth this can be quite a messy task. Personally, I have gone from total dedication to my yoga and meditation practice to total and complete aversion; though most days now I find myself somewhere in between. There are days where I feel so blissful, joyful, grateful and there are days when I feed sad, lonely, depressed. Sometimes I feel so deeply connected to everyone and everything that it overwhelms me and causes me to feel anxious. Sometimes I find myself so full of anger and rage that I can actually feel it as burning in my heart. Most days, I find my eyes simply releasing tears for no apparent reason – and with no specific emotion attached.

And yet I continue.

i continue on this path to seek the Truth of my existence because I know all the other stories of my ego-identity no longer serve me.

The pain of this resistance has a purpose: to make

us stop seeking Truth so that our ego-self may continue to exist as it is. It is our faith in something greater, the faith in the knowledge of satya that is slowly revealed to us through these practices, that keeps us strong on our path of Self-discovery.

the niYAmas

swadHYaya

[swad-HI-a-ya]

Meaning
self-observation, spiritual studies

Sutra 2:44
*By study of scriptural books
comes communion
with one's chosen deity.*

"Swa" means Atman (Brahma, God) and "adhyaya" means to study; so swadhyaya literally translates to "study of Atman (God)." To study god is to study Truth. Swadhyaya is often translated, however, as self-observation or self-study. It is the study of our ego-self, with the help of scripture, so that we can discover our true nature, the higher Self that is Atman.

So we read books on yoga. We read books on different religions and spiritual philosophy. We read the Bhagavad Gita, the Bible, Quran, etc. We seek out teachers and gurus to help us understand what we read and learn. Teachers and texts help to guide our explorations; they give us a sort of road map, if you will.

It has been said that knowing the properties of an object without ever experiencing or using it is as useless as having no knowledge about the object. For example, I know that a knife has a sharp blade and is used to cut things. But that knowledge is useless unless I have seen or used a knife. I do not know how a knife will make the job of cutting something easier for me until I have the opportunity to experience it. However, when I visit your house and you ask me to get a knife from the kitchen so I can cut my apple – something I have never seen or used before – it helps to know something about it. Knowing there is a blade with a handle and a general shape helps me to identify it and knowing it is sharp helps keep me safe from a cut. Once I use it I will also have the experience of how a knife aids me in cutting things, like my apple. So knowledge of a thing can be helpful should you encounter it someday.

Coyotes are present in various regions across North America, and they have become a bit of an issue in Southern New England (NE region of the United States) where I reside. Though they have been around here for quite a while and they have become more prevalent in densely populated areas such as suburbs and cities. I, personally, have never seen a coyote even though there have been several sightings in my neighborhood over the past few years. There are several dogs in my neighborhood; I know that coyotes resemble large dogs, and that coyotes can be aggressive when hungry or when they feel threatened. This could be useful information when I am out walking in the neighborhood and encounter what appears to be a large dog without its owner.

The same goes for studying our Selves and our true nature. It is helpful to have an idea of what we might be looking for. As we saw in the examples of the knife and coyote, having some correct knowledge is useful. I know that a coyote resembles a large dog, so if I saw an animal that resembled a Chihuahua I would not mistake it for a coyote. It is in this manner that we utilize books, sacred texts, and teachers to obtain initial information as we begin a spiritual practice.

Self-study can happen in many ways. For many yoga students it begins with their physical practice. It is on our yoga mat that we observe our physical body. We notice what it can and cannot do; we notice what we think the body can or cannot do. We notice parts of our body we never really noticed before. I remember the first time I could feel my toes. Sounds silly, I know. It was during a guided meditation during which we were lead through a body scan. Though I had participated in that meditation many times previously over several years, it was during this particular experience that I knew I had ten toes without looking at them. I could actually feel and experience each individual toe for the first time.

as we begin our self-study with our physical body it often comes with a mental dialogue. Unfortunately that dialogue is often negative. In my yoga classes I will often ask my students to observe their thoughts. To simply observe thoughts and to let them come and go in awareness, not to hold onto their story. The intent is not to move from negative to positive thoughts, though that may happen. The intent is to allow thoughts – positive or negative – to naturally arise and naturally dissipate without attachment to them.

Our responsibility as a spiritual seeker is to look for information, test it for validity via our personal experience, and either accept or deny that information as truth. Our duty is to continue to do this again and again, replacing inappropriate knowledge with appropriate knowledge as we discover it. Sometimes we simply add additional knowledge to what we already know as correct. We do this throughout our life with mundane things (or at least we should) so why should it be different with our spiritual growth?

Take fire for example. Many of us have experienced using a fire pit or having a small bon fire. We see flames, perhaps some smoke. There is a feeling of heat, maybe even a particular odor. This sits in our memory as or knowledge of "fire." The first time that you use a gas stove you may initially be taken aback when you see flames and sense a bit of heat coming from the burner. Your memory of "fire" tells you that it should not be on your stove, but as you observe further you realize that the fire is much smaller and is easy to contain so you add to your knowledge of "fire." This new knowledge informs what size fire is appropriate in different context. My husband recently witnessed a house fire. He could identify flames and smoke, even the aroma of wood burning. He could even feel the heat even though he was across the street from the house. His previous knowledge informed him that this had the markings of a "fire" but it was much larger than anything he experienced previously. His knowledge has been updated to include this new experience of "large fire." Likewise, when we discover new information about ourselves we test it through our experience. If there appears to be truth to the new information it becomes part of our knowledge of Self, either adding to our knowledge or replacing old knowledge. If truth is not found in any new information, we simply regard it as not true.

This has been my experience in writing this book. For each yama and niyama I first explored how they appeared in my life. How did I practice – or not practice – each one? What ways could I bring more of this into my daily life? My process of writing this book has been a process of self-study, of swadhyaya. Your process of reading this book may be part of *your* self-study.

This act of self-study, and in fact all yogic and spiritual practices, is to point toward our true nature, our true Selves. More accurately it is the process of eliminating the incorrect knowledge of our selves so that we can reveal correct knowledge. We do this by reading sacred texts and seeking qualified teachers help to direct our studies. But ultimately it is our own personal exploration and experimentation (using tools gained from texts and from teachers) that reveal our true Self, our higher Self. It is the revealing of our Selves as Atman.

the niYAmas

shaVAra pranIDhana
[eesh-VAH-rah pran-ED-hah-nah]

Meaning
surrender to God,
dedicating all results
and consequences of our actions to God

Sutra 2:45
***B**y total surrender to God,
Samadhi is attained.*

When I hear "surrender to God" I think of the popular phrase "let go and let god." I have heard my Christian friends say it, I have heard strangers say it, and I have seen it turned into memes on social media.

Some people use this as if to say a situation is out of their hands. It is a way of taking away the sense of responsibility – and blame – for what results from their decisions and actions. It can be an act of giving up on life, saying that you are leaving everything in god's hand – it's up to God now. Sometimes it comes from shear exhaustion and you want someone else to take care of things for a while. The definition of "surrender" supports this: "to yield to the power, control, or possession of another upon compulsion or demand;" "to give (oneself) up into the power of another" (Merriam-Webster).

I have heard yoga teachers use "surrender" during classes as an instruction to "let go" and relax in whatever pose we were in. And, up until recently, I had difficulty with using surrender in this way. What am I giving up? To whom am I surrendering? Why should I give it up? I disliked this so much that in my own classes I would use "relax," "let go," and other direct cues opposed to "surrender."

But ishvara pranidhana does not mean to surrender to god as a means of giving up or releasing responsibility.

It is letting go of our expectations, letting go of our control over desired results. Sri Swami Satchidananda states "ishvara pranidhanam is a life of dedication, of offering everything to the Lord or to humanity" (Satchidananda 149). Our actions become an offering. Our thoughts become an offering. Everything we do at any moment can become a prayer in action, and an offering to God. Not a believer in god, then offer the fruits of your actions to the greater good of humanity. Don't really like your fellow humans? Then dedicate your actions to the welfare of the earth and all its creatures. This works because the entire "world itself is God. All that is outside is God" (Satchidananda 150) and all that is within us is God.

By dedicating our actions to god/humanity, the fruits (outcomes) of our actions become an offering. By offering the fruits of our actions we are surrendering our expectations of outcome. "When we surrender our preferences to God, we remain unattached to either success or failure" (Desai 63). We go about our days performing actions and making decisions. And there may be expectations as to an outcome of those actions and decisions, but we are not attached to them. We will be okay if we don't get our way.

This surrendering takes faith. Faith that we will be okay. Faith that we will be safe. Faith that it is okay to not control everything in life. Surrendering requires us to take appropriate action at all times; and it requires us to trust that the appropriate outcome will occur. Sometimes that outcome is what we wanted, or expected. Sometimes it is not what we wanted, but we learn that it was what was appropriate at the time.

Ishvara pranidhana is not yielding to God, or giving up responsibility. In fact, it is quite the opposite. In dedicating our actions/thoughts/deeds to god and humanity, there is a responsibility on our part to ensure those actions/thoughts/deeds are appropriate for each situation. We have a responsibility to ensure that we are not intentionally causing harm to ourselves or others. We have the responsibility to act with a pure heart. When we do this and surrender all expectations, we must have faith that we will receive blessings from god/Universal Consciousness as a result. Some of these blessings come in the form of the release of stress from letting go of our attachment to expected outcomes.

Let's take the example of a young couple on a date. A young man takes his girlfriend out for a fancy dinner with the expectation that they will have sex later that evening. When they do not have sex, he becomes disappointed and perhaps even angry. If instead this young man took his girlfriend out with the sole intent of a nice dinner and enjoyable evening – yeah, sex after would be nice, but it's not a necessity – he will still have fully enjoyed the evening with or without the sex. And if they had sex, it would be a bonus not an expected outcome.

In many of the examples given throughout this

book, you can probably start to see how our attachment to expected outcomes is what causes much of our stress throughout life. By giving up this attachment, we take away some of those stressors. "All worry [and stress] is due to attachment and clinging to possessions [and people]. The attachment I mean is a mental attachment. What we want is a mental, rather than physical, detachment. We can even possess things physically if we are mentally detached. This is continuous samadhi" (Satchidananda 150).

So we can attain success, and still remain unattached. We can obtain a nice house, car, nice clothes and still remain unattached. We can have a spouse and family and remain unattached. We can achieve goals and still remain unattached. How? By giving up the expectation that we will attain success, have a nice house/car/clothes, have a family. We give up the expectation, so we do not suffer stress when we do not achieve a particular something at a particular time. We dedicate our actions as we seek to attain success and release expectation of success; success comes when it is appropriate. We dedicate our work toward buying a home and car giving up expectations of when that will happen; a nice home and car will come to us when it is appropriate. We may date many people looking for a spouse; but when we give up the expectation that "this is the one," the one we are meant to be with will come into our life at the right time.

Likewise, when we lose all our possessions in a house fire, we may eventually find less stress. Yes, there is much work to be done, yes we need to replace clothing and find a place to live, yes we are sad in the initial moments; but when we are unattached to the items we are only sad in the moment, not devastated forever. When we lose a loved one we are sad in the moment. Yes, at that time it may feel like devastation; sometimes sadness may revisit. But when we are not attached to the idea they will be with us forever, the sense of devastation is released and we are able to work through the sadness. When we can release our expectation of how life is supposed to be, we allow ourselves to live the life that we have. With this blessing, why would you not dedicate your actions to god/Universal Consciousness and the good of humanity?

Sri Swami Satchidananda mentions that this state of being mentally detached while having possessions is "continuous *samadhi*." But what is samadhi?

Samadhi is defined as the state of "contemplation…absorption" (Satchidananda 245) and "the final experience of the ultimate union of the individual soul with the cosmic soul [Universe/God]" (Desai 18). If you dive deeper into the yogic teachings, you will find that there are stages of samadhi that monks aspire to. But true samadhi is available to all of us, even if in a basic form.

"Real *samadhi* means tranquility of mind, which is possible only when we dedicate everything and are free from all attachment" (Satchidananda 150). Surrendering our attachments and expectations, dedicating our thoughts and actions to a higher power and to all of humanity takes away a level of stress so that we can experience a tranquil mind at any moment. With practice, this becomes effortless and natural. As Swami Kripalu said "actions dedicated to ourselves are useless actions and bring only pain; but actions dedicated to the Lord [and humanity] are genuine actions and bring true happiness" (Desai 64). In this manner, all our actions are truly a culmination of the yamas and niyamas in action. The aim of which is to bring a steadiness of mind, a sense of peace, and a greater knowledge of our True Nature.

*becoming***PARVATI**

İ began practicing yoga in 2002. At that time I was focused more on physical fitness and flexibility, though I also benefited from the relaxation it provided. I started, as many do, following videos at home. I attended my first studio classes after my husband purchased a class package at a local studio as a gift for me. It was at that studio that I was introduced to Amrit Yoga, but more importantly the yamas and niyamas. The teachers and staff would introduce a yama or niyamas as a theme for classes each week. I would leave each yoga class with a tiny slip of paper describing the theme for the week and an affirmation to help integrate it into my life.

I didn't get it.

fast forward to 2013 when I completed my first yoga teacher training. I took the training as an intensive, with no intention to ever teach a yoga class. We studied, among many other topics, the yamas and niyamas. I developed a much greater intellectual understanding. I could describe them and find applications of them in daily life. But I only understood them on a mental level: I got it, but still didn't get it.

In 2015, I was bestowed my spiritual name, Parvati.

I feel this "receiving a name" needs to be demystified a little bit. Each yoga tradition has a slightly different way of bestowing names. In the Kundalini yoga tradition, new teachers are bestowed their spiritual names upon teacher training graduation. I believe this may be why some people refer to them as their "yoga teacher names." In the Amrit tradition, names are given to those experienced disciples who wish to receive one. Most are yoga teachers, though some are simply long-term practitioners.

When the spiritual names are presented, our guru enters a meditative state. He looks the disciple in the eyes, connecting deeply with their soul, their Higher Self. The name is chosen based on aspects of the individual that the guru feels resonate with the name. They may be characteristics that the individual expresses at that moment, but often they are unknown to the disciple at the time. But over time and with continued study, the hidden aspects of their spiritual name become more and more apparent; and those aspects begin to integrate more fully with the individual. For me, receiving a spiritual name felt like a sort of baptism.

Parvati is kind of a big-deal name. As Hindu stories tell Parvati is the daughter of the King of the Himalayan Mountains, Himavat, and she was believed to be a reincarnation of Lord Shiva's (the god of transformation) first wife, Sati. Parvati was fascinated with Shiva from an early age and was determined to one day become his wife. As a young adult, she would spend her days tending to Shiva and his dwellings; however Shiva was so deeply immersed in his meditation practice that he hardly noticed her. After some time and many attempts to win Shiva's heart, Parvati thought the best way would be to become well-versed in the art of meditation herself. So she set off into the woods, alone.

Parvati found the most remote part of the woods, sat down, closed her eyes and began to meditate. She had only the clothes she wore; she did not eat. She had no formal training in meditation, though she had observed Shiva through the years. It was a very difficult task, but she became quite adept in the skill of meditation and deep contemplation. It was not long before word of Parvati and her devout practices reached Shiva. Very impressed with report of this young woman's feats, Shiva sought out Parvati. He questioned and tested her; hearing her answers Shiva determined that her faith was strong and her love for him pure. They wed soon after, and Shiva instructed Parvati in the teachings of yoga.

Parvati is a mother goddess, loving and nurturing. She represents devotion, and we can see that not only in her love for Shiva but also in her dedication to her meditation practice. She is strong yet feminine; and she is a creative force. Parvati is significant in the Kripalu yoga lineage because of her intimate link with Shiva. The Kripalu tradition is considered a Shiva lineage due to the worship of Shiva and his teachings. In fact, it is believed that Shiva himself incarnated in human form in order to instruct the first teacher of our lineage, Swami Kripalu.

Having such a powerful and significant name bestowed upon you, you know you're going to be in for a ride.

Upon arriving home after receiving my name, not much seemed to happen. I decided to start teaching yoga classes under this new name. Some students were excited to learn that I now had a "yoga name," and I now have several students who have never heard my birth name. I meditated most days, did my yoga postures a couple days a week. I was dedicated to this practice, but then something changed….. I stopped.

It wasn't really sudden, it happened more gradually. And the habit of not practicing soon took over. But why did I stop?

Looking back through old journals I saw a clear theme: fear. I had noticed changes and I was afraid of what that meant. I knew these changes were deep and would be completely transformational. I could already observe it in the way I was thinking; I could feel it in my body; even the way I walked felt different. My whole world was shifting and the more yoga and meditation I did, the faster that shift seemed to be moving. I knew the shift would continue, but I stopped my practice in subconscious hopes of slowing down the process of transformation.

Transformation does not work this way though. It's like cracking a raw egg into a hot pan – the egg is forever changed, it can't go back to what it was. Even if the egg is cracked into a cold pan and heated slowly, the egg will slowly transform. Furthermore, the egg can never go back to its original form inside the sealed shell. Same thing happens with yogic and spiritual practices. Once you discover something about yourself – like your True nature – you can never un-know it. You can deny it, but the knowledge will always be there. You may forget, but you cannot un-know.

So this is how my personal practice continued for about five years. Occasionally I would sit to meditate. Even less frequently I would do my yoga practice, and rarely would I attend a studio class. I continued to teach and took trainings in yoga, wellness, and nutrition. I was becoming a healer, in a sense. I left a full-time position in nutrition because it was no longer fulfilling; in fact, the stress was destroying my health. I started my own wellness business and took part-time employment. I journaled and wrote about what I was feeling and experiencing. It was not until 2018 that my next major shift took place.

As you may have guessed, the event that spurned that shift was Griffon's passing. Obviously there was grief and sadness, but my day-to-day existence was completely changed. But as you may recall from the introduction, I heard my teacher's voice saying "aparigraha" while Griffon was transitioning from life to death. This gentle nudge to "let go" turned into a push to study the yamas and niyamas. Actually, the more I ignored this nudge, the more it turned into an annoying gnawing sensation until one day I sat down and opened The Yoga Sutras of Patanjali. I began to read.

I didn't just read; I tried to understand the deeper essence and meaning. I researched sources on the internet. I asked questions and engaged discussions. I had an intellectual idea, but I still felt as though I didn't know what the yamas and niyamas were really all about. It was during advanced yoga training that I began to cultivate an understanding on a visceral level. I had knowledge, but I was now able to combine that with experience. Just as Parvati knew the conditions to successfully meditate, it was not until she actually sat down to meditate that she was able to experience – and eventually master – meditation.

As I look back on my experience of writing, the information I have shared on these pages really comes from my experience. Though I do quote sources to support what I state, the information I have shared is coming directly from my experience with each yama and niyama – not from my mind per se, but from Source. Source, Consciousness, Higher Self, God – whatever you want to call it, that is where my information, knowledge, and experience are sharing from. I have trusted that whatever comes out onto paper is exactly what needs to be shared. But I am not one to just simply trust the process. I can be the most skeptical, questioning person around. I overthink everything; and I do mean everything. To learn to be still and simply allow has been challenging, at best. And that has been part of my process: using a critical and discerning mind to deeply explore. It is through this process that I have found myself resonating more with Parvati, the name and the goddess herself.

Study and discipline are difficult. Think back to your school days and studying a difficult topic. You may have found yourself doing anything but study, just because you knew it would be difficult. But once you start, you find a pace – your groove – and stick with it. It's the same for self-study. We want to do it but avoid it at all cost because we know it will be difficult. We prioritize other tasks; find distractions over learning about ourselves. And I am no different.

I distracted myself with all sorts of things. I put all my energy into my work. I worked long days and overtime. I worked to the point of being too tired to hold a conversation with my spouse, forget the idea of doing yoga. When I left that job I found myself working an irregular schedule, which I allowed to be a barrier to my practice – notice I said "I allowed." My erratic schedule became my excuse to not meditate, to not attend yoga classes, to not look inward. I also struggled with using social media, online games, and alcohol as a means of distraction. Anything to avoid looking inward; to avoid seeking my true self. These distractions are, in part, what Patanjali referred to as "mental modifications." He relays in sutras 1.12-1.14 "these mental modifications are restrained by practice and non-attachment. Of these two, effort toward steadiness of mind is practice. Practice becomes firmly grounded when well attended to for a long time, without break and in all earnestness" (Satchidananda 18-20).

The writing of this book has become a veritable steady practice for me. I would read and study and write most days. Sometimes I found myself at a creative impasse, unable to write about what I was studying. So sometimes I would sit and meditate on the specific topic at hand. Sometimes I would look at how I was expressing or living a specific yama or niyama. Sometimes my study showed up as teaching or explaining one of these concepts to a student or friend. The steadiness of my practice was expressed in all the ways I investigated, implemented, and shared the yamas and niyamas.

So how have these practices changed me? How have the yamas and niyamas made me more like Parvati, as the book title suggests?

One of the first things I have noticed is steadiness of mind. I tend not to overreact as much as I used to. I am more able to stop my imagination from running away with all sorts of "what if" scenarios – on any event or topic. I still fall into moments of these; but they are far less frequent, and it is easier to cease those thoughts.

I have a different perspective on the world. I understand very deeply that my actions – deeds and thoughts – have a direct impact on those around me and the world at large. I also understand that the reverse is true: others actions have a direct impact on me. This is especially true for those close to me or in my geographical area, but it is also true in regards to strangers around the globe. We all have an impact on the earth and all its creatures whether we realize it or not.

 I feel a more intimate connection with nature. I have always loved being outdoors. I love smelling flowers, listening to birds. I have a natural affinity toward all sorts of animals, but especially cats. More recently I feel that connection has become deeper, that the natural world and I are not separate from each other. It has become more of a feeling than a mental understanding.

 I physically experience my environment differently. It is difficult to explain, but it is like everything and everyone is super, super close to me. It's as if we are all literally touching each other. And at the same exact time, it is as is everything is really far away. It is like I am watching all of life on a big movie screen, including watching myself.

 In studying the yamas and niyamas with earnestness over time, my understanding has deepened. I am able to transmit this information easier because of this understanding. Is there more to learn? Of course. This is only one aspect of practice and self-study, but it has brought about shifts and changes that I would not have experienced otherwise. Are there days when I fall off course? Oh yeah! I wouldn't be human if that did not happen. The difference is that I am not as hard on myself when this happens. I approach myself with more love and understanding – and, yes, that too can be a challenge.

I guess you could say that I am discovering and embracing more qualities of Parvati. A deeper compassion for others and the world. A greater dedication to self-study; learning, applying, and experiencing what I learn. Embracing the aspects of healer that I am just discovering exist within me.

*moving***FORWARD**

moving forward is more about being still than getting to a particular place or goal. It is being steady in mind each moment to moment. Practicing the yamas and niyamas helps us to cultivate that inner stillness.

What has been shared throughout this book is an interpretation of what I have, and continue, to learn. They are examples chosen because I felt they would be relatable. This does not mean that the examples I shared are the only ways the yamas and niyamas can be experienced. In fact, the yamas and niyamas permeate every aspect of life. The more you study them, the more apparent this becomes.

The yamas and niyamas do not exist in their own little bubbles, however. They work in harmony with each other simultaneously. You may concentrate on one and in doing so the others are learned and expanded upon as well. Likewise, they do not exist separate from the other six limbs of yoga (asana, pranayama, dharana, dyana, and Samadhi). Practicing one leads to the ability to experience the others. Learning and practicing the yamas are not linear either. They build upon each other no matter what order you learn and explore them.

That being said, I recommend re-reading this book often. Take your time to explore each yama and niyama individually. Journal about it, observe it in yourself, observe how others exhibit it – or don't. Find ways that you can embrace and embody more of these observances. And repeat as much as necessary. Read and explore other spiritual and religious texts. Look for similarities, not just differences. Explore how they may simply be different expressions of the same concepts. This is the approach I took in preparation for this book.

What makes the yamas and niyamas special, in my opinion, is that they are a roadmap for ethical behavior. It is one aspect of a yogic lifestyle, and they can be implemented with or without a physical asana (posture) practice. They are universal; applicable to people of all faiths, all ethnicities, and all walks of life. The benefit of studying and practicing these precepts is that they help you to gradually become more aware of your true essence, your True Self, and your connectedness to all beings.

With steady, consistent practice layers of truth are revealed to the seeker. With each layer that is removed, there becomes a need to dive back into the lesson to learn a bit more. Take aparigraha for example. The first lesson to learn may be that you realize you have way too many things in your home that you do not need. So you begin to clear away broken items and things you no longer use.

You study more about aparigraha and realize you are keeping clothes that do not fit you, so you clear out the closets and donate the clothing. You re-examine aparigraha and discover an attachment to sentimental items. Your job title changes (but not the actual work) and you discover an attachment to that title and what it conveyed about you and your role. This type of study, observance, and application continues to include more things, ideas, relationships, and beliefs – all sorts of things that we did not previously realize we have attachments to. Of course this is only one simple example, but it illustrates that study, application, and re-examination of these principles are an on-going process.

You can image climbing up a spiral staircase. As you complete one full circle, you have returned near the starting mark, just a floor higher. It is familiar but yet your perspective has changed, perhaps there is something new to see that wasn't visible from the floor below. It is revisiting a lesson with new knowledge and perspective. The process of spiritual contemplation is like the process of climbing a spiral staircase.

What comes next for me, you may be asking me. How will I move forward? The same as I recommend for you: continue to study, to apply, to re-examine, and repeat. My study has not ended because I wrote a book. In fact, my earnest study has only just begun.

In all faiths, spiritual teachings have been passed from teacher to disciple/student for centuries; often the student becomes a teacher as well. Majority of these teachers were renunciates – priests, monks, and holy people – who spent countless hours each day in prayer, meditation, and contemplation in efforts to reach spiritual liberation. This is who formal teachings were intended for. A less rigorous version was recommended for householders like you and me – everyday people working and raising families.

"Practice becomes firmly grounded when well attended to for a long time, without break and in all earnestness. The consciousness of self-mastery in one who is free from craving for objects seen or heard about is non-attachment. When there is no thirst for even the gunas (constituents of Nature) due to the realization of the Purusha (true Self), that is Supreme non-attachment" (Satchidananda 19-28). This Supreme non-attachment comes from an understanding that we do not need to 'obtain" anything because we are already it/already have it – everything is connected, we are all one.

Study of the yamas and niyamas are the practice which leads to steadiness of mind. This steadiness of mind creates the environment that leads to self-awareness (of our True Nature). Self- awareness is the Supreme non-attachment.

To be honest, I sometimes think it would be easier to be a monk. Isolated from all the distractions that feed our ego mind; fully dedicated to spiritual pursuits. Of course I know, in reality, it is not any easier just a different experience. It sometimes seems like it would be easier without the perceived distractions of jobs, family, society and their perceived demands upon us, to be able to pursue spiritual study without distraction.

Well, I don't know about you, but I'm not joining a monastery anytime soon. I will continue to study, to observe. I will study and live in these teachings – specifically the yamas and niyamas – to the best of my ability so that I may live in greater and greater alignment with Truth. So that I may live in greater attunement to the expressions of Parvati as they appear in my life; and to embrace the expressions of Parvati that my guru saw in me.

And I invite you to do the same – again and again and again… To study, observe, apply, and repeat for each of the yamas and niyamas. May this study – this practice – lead you to the realization and the awakening of your true Nature, your Purusha (Universal Consciousness, God).

RESOURCES

Becker, Suzie. (1990). *All I need to know I learned from My Cat*. New York, NY: Workman Publishing.

Desai, Amrit. (2010). *Amrit Yoga and the Yoga Sutras*. Salt Springs, FL: Yoga Network International.

Frawley, Dr. David. (1996). *Ayurveda and the Mind: The Healing of Consciousness*. Twin Lakes, WI: Lotus Press.

Lad, Vasant. (2002). *Textbook of Ayurveda, Volume 1*. Albuquerque, NM: Ayurvedic Press.

Lad, Vasant. (2007). *Textbook of Ayurveda, Volume 2*. Albuquerque, NM: Ayurvedic Press.

Merriam-Webster. (2018). Merriam-Webster.com

Satchidananda, Sri Swami. (2011). *The Yoga Sutras of Patanjali*. Buckingham, VA: Integral Yoga Publications.

Snelling, John. (1991). *The Buddhist Handbook*. Rochester, NY: Inner Traditions International, LTD.

ABOUT THE AUTHOR
Julie A. Hillman, MS NDTR RYT

Julie works as a Holistic Wellness/Nutrition Consultant and Yoga Teacher in Rhode Island. She holds degrees in nutrition and social work, and is an Ayurvedic Consultant. She has been leading yoga classes since becoming certified in 2013 and has taught under her spiritual name, Parvati, since it was bestowed in 2015. In addition to interests in yoga and wellness, she is an avid kayaker and has been known to participate in charity 5k races from time to time. She is pictured here with her cat, Griffon.

To learn more about Julie and her services, visit **www.satya-wellness.com**

Manufactured by Amazon.ca
Acheson, AB